A Year of Celebration:

Experiencing God through the Feast Days of the Church

Patricia Mitchell

Editor

The Word Among Us Press
9639 Doctor Perry Road
Ijamsville, Maryland 21754
www.wau.org

ISBN: 0-932085-54-7

Cover design by Christopher Ranck and David Crosson
Cover photograph by Harriet Wise

Made and printed in the United States of America.

TABLE OF CONTENTS

Introduction

When was the last time you gathered together with family and friends for a celebration? It could have been a baptism, anniversary, wedding, or special birthday. Whatever the occasion, the day is probably etched in your memory in a deeper way than if you had not made a conscious effort to commemorate the event. Celebrations punctuate our lives and imbue them with meaning and joy. They allow us to take time out from our own busy schedules to come together to express our love for one other.

In the same way, we come together as a church family to celebrate those special events that make us who we are—the people of God. First and foremost, feast days commemorate God's intervention into human history. For that reason, Easter is the highest holy day of the church, the day when through his resurrection, Jesus conquered sin and death forever. In fact, every Sunday is a feast day, a special day set aside for the community of believers to recall the paschal mystery. Other feasts honor the apostles, martyrs, and saints who spread the gospel and built the church.

More than a Calendar of Events. These days are filled with treasures that we can uncover if we pause long enough to look for them. At first glance, the liturgical year appears to be simply a calendar of events, but as we participate in each celebration, we will find that it is much more. Through this structure, God invites us to receive his abundant graces. As the title of the book implies, our goal at The Word Among Us Press in developing *A Year of Celebration: Experiencing God through the Feast Days of the Church* is to have our readers draw closer to the Lord by experiencing his constant and loving presence in their lives within the context of the liturgical year.

One of the ways we can enter into the joy of these feasts is through the liturgy. At Mass, the Scripture readings help us to see how our celebration is rooted in God's word. Through the Eucharist, we unite ourselves with everyone in the body who is also celebrating the same feast. As we reflect on the Scriptures and receive the Eucharist, we can remember that Catholics all over the world are doing the same thing. Together, our prayer rises to God "as incense before thee" (Psalm 141:2).

In our own times of prayer on these days, we can seek to understand God's plan for humanity as well as his specific plan for our lives. Although each feast celebrates an event that occurred a long time ago, it still has significance for us today. By devoting extra time to prayer on these special days, we can find out what meaning the feast has for us here and now, as Christians living in the twenty-first century.

For example, the feast of the Triumph of the Cross helps us to meditate on the role of the cross in our own lives. The Transfiguration can affect our views about the resurrection and life after death. The experience of the first apostles at Pentecost can give us a desire for a greater outpouring of the Holy Spirit. All these mysteries of our faith are relevant to modern-day Christians because Christ has risen and lives among us.

Unwrapping a Gift. When we dig a little deeper into our hearts on the church's holy days, God can show us where we need to change. He can free us from our doubts and fears, fill us with hope, and cover us with his love. Each feast day is a gift for us to unwrap. The Lord wants us to have these gifts to help us to live more fully his life in us. As you take the time to pray through the meditations in this book along with the additional questions and points that follow each meditation, we hope you will find yourself challenged, refreshed, and more intimately united with Jesus.

A *Year of Celebration* includes every feast where the Scripture passages change from the continuous sequence of the weekday or Sunday lectionary readings to readings that are specific for that day. In order to better understand the framework of the liturgical calendar, the following information may be helpful:

- Solemnities, such as Easter and Christmas, are the highest holy days of the church. These days sometimes have separate readings for vigil Masses.

- Feasts, such as the Presentation of the Lord on February 2 or the Birth of Mary on September 8, are next in importance. The days on which the apostles are honored, along with the early martyrs, are also feasts.

- Memorials are reserved for honoring well-known saints or martyrs. Some memorials can be celebrated at the option of the local diocese, while others are obligatory. For memorials included in *A Year of Celebration*, the church has skipped the usual lectionary sequence to use Scripture readings that have a specific meaning or significance for that saint.

For some holy days, such as the Baptism of the Lord, the gospel readings change depending on the cycle of readings for that year. Cycle A readings, which will be used in 2002, are from Matthew's Gospel; cycle B readings, which will be used in 2003, are from Mark's Gospel; and cycle C readings, in use for 2001, rely on Luke's Gospel.

Some feasts, such as Easter, are "moveable"—that is, the date on which they are celebrated changes from year to year. This dictates when subsequent feasts such as the Ascension and Pentecost will be celebrated. Fixed feasts, like Christmas, are always celebrated on the same date. *A Year of Celebration* has attempted to arrange all the feasts in chronological order, but from year to year, this order could change slightly, as when Easter is celebrated early or late.

The sanctoral is the calendar of saints' feasts and memorials. The Second Vatican Council wanted to ensure that these feasts did not take precedence over the feasts that commemorate the mysteries of salvation, and so reforms were made to reduce the number of days on which saints and martyrs would be honored by the universal church. Only saints "who are truly of universal importance" (*Constitution on the Sacred Liturgy*, 111) are celebrated by the entire church.

Many feasts and holy days honor the Blessed Virgin Mary. The Fathers of Vatican II explained that because Mary "is inseparably linked with her son's saving work," the church "admires the most excellent fruit of redemption, and joyfully contemplates, as in a faultless image, that which she herself desires and hopes wholly to be" (*Constitution on the Sacred Liturgy*, 103).

We have a God who each and every day gives us his word in Scripture, his body and blood in the Eucharist, and his comfort and peace in prayer. "This is the day which the Lord has made; let us rejoice and be glad in it" (Psalm 118:24). Let us take up every day the Lord gives to us with eagerness, expectancy, and an open heart, ready to receive God's overflowing mercy and grace.

Patricia Mitchell
Editor
The Word Among Us Press

JANUARY 1

Mary, Mother of God

Solemnity

Numbers 6:22-27
Psalm 67:2-3,5-6,8
Galatians 4:4-7
Luke 2:16-21

The LORD lift up his countenance upon you, and give you peace. (Numbers 6:26)

The title "Mother of God" is the Western church's equivalent of the ancient Eastern title Theotokos, which means "God-bearer." In 431, the Council of Ephesus sanctioned the title Theotokos for Mary as a way of declaring and protecting the divinity of Christ. The title declares the most important truth about Mary: She is the Mother of God.

When we celebrate this feast, we honor not only Mary but Jesus, true God and true man. We proclaim the glorious truth that in Mary's womb the Second Person of the Trinity united himself completely with our humanity. "Taking a body like our own, because all our bodies were liable to . . . death, he surrendered his body to death in place of all. . . . Through this union of the immortal Son of God with our human nature, all were clothed with incorruption" (St. Athanasius, *On the Incarnation*, 8,9).

In Mary, we see the portrait of one who knew God's shining face upon her, filling her with grace (Numbers 6:25). Looking upon her with love and showering her with divine blessings, God prepared her to say "yes" to his plan that she bear his Son into this world. As Mary consented in faith, the Father gave her his peace (6:26), continually encouraging her to trust him as she saw his plan unfold. How deeply she must have needed this peace, as she faced dangerous and frightening circumstances such as giving birth in a faraway city in a cave, or fleeing to Egypt in the dead of night (Luke 2:4-7; Matthew 2:13-15). In each situation, Mary learned to trust more fully that God would bless her and keep her (Numbers 6:24).

Because the Son of God took flesh in Mary's womb, we too can share in these glorious blessings. We have been baptized into Christ; we have a share in his humanity. We are heirs of the blessings that God gave to Israel and in a particular way to Mary, the beloved Daughter of Zion.

Like Mary, we can walk confidently in the blessing and peace of the Lord. The Son of God, who left his throne to become one like us, has conquered sin and death for all of us. Each day, we can freely receive the life of Jesus into our hearts simply by responding "yes" to the Lord's call, just as Mary did. By Jesus' sanctifying blood, we have been made vessels of the Holy Spirit, enabling us to cry out "Abba! Father!" as true sons and daughters of God (Galatians 4:6-7). The Lord is not far off, but very near; indeed he dwells within us through his Holy Spirit. Let us turn to him and allow his blessing, grace, and mercy to shine upon us.

Points for Meditation:

- As Mother of God, Mary bore Jesus into this world. Now, as Jesus' sisters and brothers (Mark 3:35), we are called to follow Mary's example and bring the life and love of God to others. How can we be "God-bearers" to our families, our coworkers, our friends? How can we bear Christ into a needy world?

- Mary was open to God's call for her life. Is there something specific God is calling you to do? Have you responded with Mary's "yes"? If not, what is holding you back?
- Do you feel an inner peace that comes from God? Is there something in your life that makes you feel less than peaceful? If so, can you identify it? Are there steps you can take to alleviate any anxiety you may be feeling?

Prayer:

Holy Spirit, come into my life deeply and powerfully this year. Fill me with Jesus and his words, as you filled Mary. Help me to live and proclaim the gospel of Jesus.

Epiphany of the Lord

Solemnity

(Celebrated on the Sunday between January 2 and January 8)

Isaiah 60:1-6
Psalm 72:1-2,7-8,10-13
Ephesians 3:2-3,5-6
Matthew 2:1-12

Nations shall come to your light, and kings to the brightness of your rising. (Isaiah 60:3)

Picture an apple seed planted in the dark, cold ground—seemingly dead. At the right moment, however, nourished by the sun and rain, it bursts forth into the light of day. As the seed grows and matures into a tree, it delights our senses with the beauty of its branches, the fragrance of its blossoms, the taste of its fruit, the shade of its leaves.

So it was for Jerusalem at the time of this prophecy. The holy city had been destroyed by

Nebuchadnezzar's army; it lay in ruins during the long years of the Babylonian exile. Yet in the midst of this darkness, Yahweh spoke prophetically about what he would do: make Jerusalem a light that would attract the Gentiles to God.

In a similar way, Jesus' birth was the dawn of a glorious light, yet as an infant he did not look all that powerful or resplendent. He was born in the darkness of a stable without any fanfare. Only a few recognized him. Among these "few" were the wise men who were led to Jesus by God's revelation. These emissaries from the East stand in Scripture as representatives of the "nations" who would at last come to the light of God.

"Epiphany" is a Greek word meaning "manifestation." What was manifested or made clear to the wise men who came from the East to worship the Jewish Messiah? They knew that they were somehow included in the promise of this one who was "born king of the Jews" (Matthew 2:2). These wise men were Gentile, not Jewish. They were the first fulfillment of what was proclaimed in the letter to the Ephesians: With the coming of Jesus, the Jewish Messiah, God was inviting the Gentiles to be part of his people (Ephesians 3:5-6).

Today, this prophecy from the Book of Isaiah continues to realize its fulfillment as the church is called to "arise" and "shine" (Isaiah 60:1), drawing everyone from all nations to Christ. Yet even in her current state, the church is only a shadow of what God has in store for her! Even the most glorious aspects of the church are dark compared with the light that will shine upon it when Jesus returns to take his church—all his people—into his kingdom.

Let us pray for the church, asking the Spirit that the light of God's glory would shine through the people of God and reflect Christ to all the earth. Let us pray that we will welcome Christ into our hearts every day, allowing his light to penetrate us and conquer any darkness within us. Both as individuals and as members of the church, we can reflect the glory of God in our lives.

Points for Meditation:

- God drew the Magi to his Son with a compelling sign, a brilliant new star in the night sky. What compelling signs has God used in your life to draw you closer to him?

- The Magi recognized Jesus, the Son of God, as a small baby in a humble setting. Recall a specific situation in which you recognized the presence of Jesus. What was it that made you "see" Christ?
- God wants to save all his people and bring them into his body, the church. Intercede on behalf of church leaders and for all members of the church, that they would be inspired to commit themselves to the work of building the kingdom. Pray especially for your own parish.

Prayer:

Lord, let the seed of your grace in us blossom into your perfect plan for your church. May we reflect this plan more fully each day so that your glory will shine to all the nations.

Baptism of the Lord

Feast

(Celebrated on the Sunday after January 6)

Isaiah 42:1-4,6-7
Psalm 29:1-4,9-10
Acts 10:34-38
Cycle A: Matthew 3:13-17
Cycle B: Mark 1:7-11
Cycle C: Luke 3:15-16,21-22

"This is my beloved Son,
with whom I am well pleased."
(Matthew 3:17)

Why did Jesus, the Sinless One, submit himself to John's baptism of repentance? At his baptism, Jesus accepted his mission as God's suffering servant on behalf of all sinful men and women. By submitting humbly to John's baptism, Jesus gave us a foreshadowing of the "baptism" of his bloody death on the cross, where out of love he gave his life for the remission of our sins (Mark 10:38,45).

Because Jesus humbled himself so completely, his Father proclaimed how delighted he was in him (Mark 1:11). The Holy Spirit, too, was present, anointing Jesus for the work he was about to begin. At his baptism, Jesus became the source of the Spirit for all who would believe in him. The heavens were opened, the Spirit fell, and a new creation was inaugurated.

If we want to experience the power and grace of this new creation in our lives, we must follow Jesus' example. St. Gregory of Nazianzus, a fourth-century church Father, gives us this advice: "Let us be buried with Christ by baptism, in order to rise with him. Let us go down with him in order to be raised with him. Let us rise with him in order to be glorified with him." If we want to experience the transformation Gregory wrote about, we need to ask the Holy Spirit to forge the same humility in our hearts that Jesus showed at his baptism.

Jesus is ever ready to renew us in his Spirit and to anoint us for our mission. He wants to make us "light" and "salt" to those around us (Matthew 5:13,14). He wants his love and truth to shine through us so that others will be touched by his goodness. Ask the Lord to fill you with his Holy Spirit so that you may radiate the joy of the gospel to those around you. As you do, heaven will open for you as well.

Points for Meditation:

- We who have been baptized into Christ have received the same Spirit as Jesus. We too can hear the Father say of us, "This is my beloved." Imagine yourself in the Jordan River being baptized with Jesus. Ask the Holy Spirit to manifest his power in you in a fresh way.
- Jesus humbled himself by submitting to John's baptism of repentance. How does humility in our own lives help us to better love and serve the Lord? Is there a specific area in your life where you need to grow in humility?
- Baptized into his life and death, we can take on the character, and even the very heart, of Jesus. Ask the Lord to give you the faith to believe this truth. Then ask him to open your heart and transform you into his image.

Prayer:

Lord, fill me with your Holy Spirit. May I find joy in seeking to please you, just as you found joy in seeking to please your Father.

JANUARY 25

Conversion of St. Paul

Feast

Acts 22:3-16 or Acts 9:1-22
Psalm 117:1-2
Mark 16:15-18

Suddenly a light from heaven flashed about him. And he fell to the ground and heard a voice saying to him, "Saul, Saul, why do you persecute me?" (Acts 9:3-4)

What an extraordinary turn of events! In Jerusalem, Saul had murder in his heart for Christians. Yet, by the time he arrived in Damascus, he was ready to become one of the boldest and most zealous Christians the world has known.

What caused such a transformation? It was nothing less than a dramatic encounter with the risen Lord Jesus. As Saul was on the road toward

Damascus, the glory of the Lord flashed about him like a blinding light and struck him to the ground. Then Jesus personally spoke to Saul in such a way that he would never be the same again. This experience was so powerful that Saul was temporarily blinded and needed the prophetic ministry of a Christian named Ananias to restore his sight.

If Jesus can so radically change an enemy and persecutor of the church as vehement as Saul, think of what he can do in us—people who are already members of his body and washed clean in the waters of baptism! God wants to make us fully alive in his Spirit. He wants to so fill us with his life that we would naturally manifest the joy of knowing Jesus personally and demonstrate to others the vitality of his life. Each one of us is capable of knowing Jesus just as deeply as Paul did, and experiencing his life and his power. This same Jesus who personally touched Saul is ready and able to transform each of us, setting us on fire with his love.

The keys to receiving more of the Lord and the power of his life are to hunger for him, strive to obey his word, and simply ask for more. In every age, countless Christians can testify to having encountered Jesus in a new and powerful way, such that their lives changed dramatically. Many, like Saul, have been radically transformed and empowered for some role of service as part of the mission of the body of Christ. This power of the risen Lord is available to each of us. Let us ask him, even beg him, to touch us afresh so that we will be greatly changed. Jesus can do it!

Points for Meditation:

- Do you believe that Jesus wants to give you more of his power and life? Spend some time renouncing any doubts and fears you may have, and then ask him to fill you with more of him.
- From the moment of Paul's conversion, prayer became his constant companion (Acts 9:11). In one of his letters, Paul urged his Christian brother and sisters to "pray constantly" (1 Thessalonians 5:17). Is daily prayer a priority in your life? What are some ways you can improve your prayer life?
- When Jesus asked Paul, "Why do you persecute me?" (Acts 9:4), he was indicating that an attack against his loved ones is also an assault against him. We are members of Jesus' body, joined to him. When we slander a brother or sister in Christ, we hurt Jesus. Repent of any

times you may have ridiculed or attacked a fellow member of Christ's body.

Prayer:

Lord Jesus, I ask for a deeper touch of your power and your glory. I know you will never fail me. Change me radically, Lord, so that I might love you and serve you all the days of my life.

JANUARY 26

Sts. Timothy and Titus, bishops

Memorial

First reading:
2 Timothy 1:1-8 or
Titus 1:15

Do not be ashamed of testifying to our Lord, nor of me his prisoner, but take your share of suffering for the gospel in the power of God. (2 Timothy 1:8)

References to Timothy and Titus—and the important roles they played in spreading the gospel and caring for the infant church—are sprinkled throughout the New Testament. From these passages, we know that St. Paul had great confidence in the ability of these two disciples to accomplish the work of bringing the good news to the gentile world.

Titus was a Greek whom Paul called his "partner and fellow worker" (2 Corinthians 8:23). He accompanied Paul on his second visit to Jerusalem (Galatians 2:1) and, after a visit to Corinth, brought comforting news to Paul about the renewed zeal of the church there (2 Corinthians 7:5-7). Paul assured the Corinthians that Titus earnestly cared for them (8:16). Eventually Titus became the leader of the church in Crete.

Timothy was Paul's "beloved and faithful child in the Lord" (1 Corinthians 4:17). The son of a Jewish mother and Greek father whom Paul met at Lystra (Acts 16:1-3), Timothy accompanied Paul on many of his missions and also was sent as Paul's emissary to several of the Christian communities (1 Thessalonians 3:2,6; 1 Corinthians 16:10). Paul was deeply grateful for Timothy and his service, telling the Philippians "how as a son with a father he has served with me in the gospel (Philippians 2:22). Timothy was eventually named bishop of Ephesus.

The churches that Timothy and Titus oversaw had their difficulties. Instead of requesting easier assignments, however, these men understood that they were to persevere in teaching and loving their congregations and that God would do the rest. Like Jesus' parable of the sower and the seed (Mark 4:1-20), they had to sow God's word without looking back to see if their work was bearing fruit.

Having accepted the gospel, we, like Timothy, Titus, and Paul, are called to sow seeds of the kingdom wherever we go. Many people we speak with about Jesus simply will not hear the gospel, and some who do hear it will not accept it. Worrying about where the seed of our work for God falls, however, is not our concern. Our charge is to share the gospel and let God give it the growth he intends.

Like these saints, we too must "stick with it" as we tell those around us about Jesus. We must show all the love and compassion of Jesus and stay with those in need of the gospel—no matter how well or poorly they seem to be receiving it. It is in times of hardship and testing that real seeds of faith are sown and the real fruit of Christianity is borne. Let us all take up our calling. It's not just for pastors, but for parents, spouses, and neighbors as well.

Points for Meditation:

- Paul exhorted Timothy to "rekindle" the gift of God that was within him (2 Timothy 1:6). Ask the Lord today to rekindle the fire of his love within you.
- Timothy and Titus persevered in the work that God had given to them. Is there any work that God has given to you that you are tempted to abandon? If so, ask the Lord to help you re-dedicate yourself to that mission.
- Timothy, Titus, and Paul were united in a deep love for Christ and for one another. Ask the Lord to give you a deep love for your family and friends, one that is divinely inspired. Pray for unity in your family, in your parish, and in the church.

Prayer:

Lord, you called Timothy and Titus to serve the church. May their example and prayers help us to continue the task of building and strengthening your church, so that on your return, you will indeed find faith on earth.

FEBRUARY 2

Presentation of the Lord

Feast

Malachi 3:1-4
Psalm 24:7-10
Hebrews 2:14-18
Luke 2:22-40

The Lord whom you seek will suddenly come to his temple. (Malachi 3:1)

In first-century Palestine, Jewish families brought their firstborn son to the temple forty days after his birth to consecrate him to God. At the same time, the mother was ritually purified after childbirth. Joseph and Mary took Jesus to the temple to carry out these rituals, where they offered the sacrifice of the poor—a pair of turtle-doves or two young pigeons. Under the inspiration of the Holy Spirit, two elderly people, Simeon and Anna, were waiting for them.

If you were a pious Jew in the temple that day, what would you see? A poor couple with a little baby—one of many being presented to the Lord. Would you recognize this child as the Messiah? Only Simeon and Anna did. Not even the priest who accepted the parents' sacrifice could see who Jesus was. It seems that those who recognized Jesus were the ones who spent time pondering God's word in their hearts and asking for wisdom to understand his ways.

The feast of the Presentation challenges us to ask whether we recognize Jesus as he moves in our lives. Every day, Jesus wants to come into our hearts and shine the light of God's love and mercy. Every day, he wants to claim us as his dwelling place and establish his presence as our greatest treasure. Like Simeon and Anna, we will be sensitive to his movements as we spend time in prayer, quieting our minds and loving God with our hearts.

Our Father, who delights in sharing with us the treasures of his kingdom, asks only that we come to him humbly. He asks us to empty ourselves, so that there is room in our lives for his grace. In order to receive the things of heaven, we must divest ourselves of the things of earth. He is a righteous God and will not share his glory with another. He will reveal himself to us as we make our hearts available to him. And then he will be the delight of our hearts.

Points for Meditation:

- How can you better prepare yourself for your encounter with the Lord? Think of where you most likely will meet Jesus—in the poor and lonely, the sick and dying, and in his temple, in the Eucharist. How will you welcome him?
- On the day that Mary and Joseph brought Jesus to the temple, he was less than six weeks old. Imagine yourself as Simeon or Anna, taking the baby Jesus in your arms and loving him in advance for the sacrifice he would make for you by dying on the cross.
- Simeon prophesied that because of Jesus, "the thoughts out of many hearts may be revealed" (Luke 2:35). Ask Jesus to illuminate the deepest recesses of your hearts. Where you find darkness, ask him to cleanse you with his blood.

Prayer:

Lord Jesus, I welcome you. I am grateful for your sacrifice, which enables me to receive your presence. I empty myself of the things of this world and place myself before your throne. Holy Spirit, come and fill me with wisdom.

FEBRUARY 22

Chair of St. Peter

Feast

1 Peter 5:1-4
Psalm 23:1-6
Matthew 16:13-19

You are Peter, and on this rock I will build my church. (Matthew 16:18)

The feast of the Chair of Peter has been celebrated from the earliest times by the church at Rome, first on January 18 in recognition of the day when Peter is said to have held his first service with the Roman faithful, and since the Middle Ages, on February 22—traditionally considered the anniversary of Peter's proclamation of Jesus as Messiah.

The feast recalls Peter's authority as the head of the apostles, as well as the authority of all those who succeed Peter. In early Christian times, bishops had official chairs on which they sat as they preached and taught their people. Over time, the chair of a bishop came to be viewed as a symbol of his authority and has been regarded with great respect.

Jesus told Peter that he was the "rock" upon which he would build his church, and that Peter would be given "the keys of the kingdom of heaven" (Matthew 16:18-19). Consequently, to Peter and his successors is accorded a primacy over the church. The Chair of St. Peter has come to represent the pope's special calling to teach and serve the people of God.

Why did Jesus choose Peter over his other disciples to become the "rock" on which to build his church? After all, while Peter often did make bold statements of faith, he also contradicted himself—even shortly afterwards. Following his proclamation of Jesus as Messiah, for instance, Peter pleaded with Jesus not to go to Jerusalem. Because of his lack of understanding of what was to occur on the cross, Peter was rebuked by Jesus (Matthew 16:21-23). Then, at the Last Supper, Peter assured Jesus that he would rather die than deny him; yet that very night Peter denied him (Mark 14:29-31,66-72).

Was Peter's leadership given to him because of his great performance? Evidently not. What Jesus recognized in Peter was his faith. Yes, Peter's passionate attachment to Jesus led him to make promises he could not keep, but he was determined to believe. After every failing, he ran back to Jesus for forgiveness and restoration. It is this attachment to Jesus—this reliance on him at all costs—that made Peter the "rock" on which Jesus built his entire church.

Passionate attachment to Jesus pleases our Father in heaven. Like Peter, we will sometimes fail to live up to our promises or to do what is right. The most important thing, however, is our attitude and our willingness to turn to God for forgiveness each time we sin. We may see only our unbelief and failings, but Jesus sees the desires of our hearts. Let us look to Peter as an example of faith. Jesus can use even the weakest people to build his church, as long as they respond to his grace of faith.

Points for Meditation

- What is it about Peter's faith that is most attractive to you? Ask the Lord to give you the same faith that made Peter cling to Jesus at all times.
- How do you react when you become aware of a sin in your life? If you are tempted to become

discouraged, ask the Lord to give you the wisdom to see these temptations for what they are and the strength to overcome them.

- As successors to Peter and the apostles, our church leaders are called to tend the flock of God willingly and humbly. As Jesus prayed for Peter, let us pray for our pope and for all the bishops, that the Lord would continue to guide the church by his Spirit.

Prayer:

Lord, we pray for all whose faith is wavering. Bring them to greater intimacy with you. Let us not be discouraged by our failings, but ever more determined to believe.

Ash Wednesday

Joel 2:12-18
Psalm 51:3-6,12-14,17
2 Corinthians 5:20–6:2
Matthew 6:1-6,16-18

We beseech you on behalf of Christ, be reconciled to God. (2 Corinthians 5:20)

As we begin this holy season of Lent, St. Paul's blessed invitation can set the tone for our preparation of Easter. Paul's appeal to be reconciled with God has echoed across the centuries. The ashes we receive at Mass this day—a sign of our repentance—date back sixteen hundred years, when sinners publicly expressed their sorrow for their sin.

Why do we begin Lent with a spirit of repentance? God our Father respects the freedom he has given us as his creatures. He asks, entreats, and invites us to draw near to him, rending our hearts, and not our garments (Joel 2:13), in true repentance and desire for reconciliation. He encourages us to have the attitude of the psalmist, acknowledging our sin and

God's justice, and bringing the acceptable sacrifice of a broken and contrite heart (Psalm 51:16-17).

How do we accomplish this? How do we respond to God's invitation in an attitude of humble repentance? The truth is that God does not demand that we perform acts of piety merely to be seen by others. He doesn't expect us to make ourselves holier. He knows that on our own, we can't. Only God can enable us to say "yes" to him in our hearts. The Father made Jesus Christ, his sinless and perfect Son, "to be sin," so that his redemption could penetrate into the darkest, most isolated part of our experience, so that we can become "the righteousness of God" (2 Corinthians 5:21). Our lives can be filled with the holiness of God, raised above the limitations and impotence of a humanity darkened by sin. What a great and glorious gift our heavenly Father offers us, bringing new life and an ever-increasing desire for deeper fellowship with God!

Let us not receive this gift in vain, or let his invitation fall on deaf ears. The appeal that St. Paul made centuries ago resounds today. "Now is the acceptable time; now is the day of salvation" (2 Corinthians 6:2). Our human cooperation is necessary if the power of the gospel is to be effective in our own lives and in the church. May our Lenten practices, meant to demonstrate our response to God, succeed in disposing us toward humility and receptivity.

Points for Meditation:

- Take up God's invitation to "rend your heart" (Joel 2:13) this Lent by examining your conscience. Ask the Lord to show you areas of sin that are blocking his love. Celebrate the Sacrament of Reconciliation and rejoice in God's mercy.
- Prayer, fasting, and alsmgiving—the traditional practices of Lent—help us turn away from the things that so easily distract us. Pray about how you think the Lord wants you to take up these practices during Lent so that you can focus on him more intensely.
- Is there one area or pattern of sin in your life that continues to plague you? Ask the Lord to give you a victory in this area over the Lenten season.

Prayer:

Heavenly Father, with the freedom you have given us, we say "yes" to your invitation! We long to be fully reconciled to you and to participate in your holiness. Make each day of Lent be a new "day of salvation" for us, bringing us a deeper knowledge and experience of your life.

MARCH 19

St. Joseph, husband of Mary

Solemnity

2 Samuel 7:4-5,12-14,16
Psalm 89:2-5,27,29
Romans 4:13,16-18,22
Matthew 1:16,18-21,24 or Luke 2:41-51

When Joseph woke from sleep, he did as the angel of the Lord commanded him; he took his wife. (Matthew 1:24)

All glory to you, Father, for your humble servant, St. Joseph. He was a truly righteous man, in whom there was no hypocrisy. At all times he followed your will, upholding your word by his every action.

All glory to you, Father, for revealing your will to Joseph. You spoke to him in dreams, just as you spoke to our spiritual ancestors, the Old Testament patriarchs. Called to be the guardian of the

Redeemer, Joseph was another Abraham, the father of our faith. Like Abraham, he hoped against hope and trusted in you, even in the most difficult situations. From him you received the absolute trust that you value so highly in believers' hearts. Just as Abraham trusted that you could bring Isaac back from the dead, Joseph reasoned that you, O God, are the master of the impossible. He trusted you in the impossible dilemma of Mary's pregnancy, and as he waited and relied upon you, you overcame his doubt, and replaced it with faith. You overcame his despair, and replaced it with hope.

All glory to you, Father, for the obedience of your servant Joseph. To fulfill your will, he humbly took Mary to be his wife and welcomed your Son into his home and into his heart. You taught Joseph to be a man of decision and determination as he cared for and protected the mother and child. With deep humility and faith, he guided your Son, Jesus, as he grew in wisdom and in the Spirit. By adoption into Joseph's lineage, Jesus became a true son of David; by his zeal for your will, Joseph showed that, like David, he was a man after God's own heart. How fitting that he would be entrusted with the Savior!

Points for Meditation:

- Joseph, like Abraham before him, believed God. "In hope he believed against hope" (Romans 4:18). Faith like this comes only as a gift of God. Is there a situation in your life now—or in the life of someone you love—that requires you to "hope against hope"? If so, ask God to give you the faith of Abraham and Joseph. Then wait in joyful expectancy for that gift.
- God called Joseph to be the husband of Mary and the foster father of the Messiah. He also gave Joseph the grace to carry out his mission. Think of the times in your life when grace enabled you to carry out something difficult but necessary. Thank God for all the times in the past he has given you the grace to be obedient, and ask him to continue to pour out his grace upon you.
- On this feast of St. Joseph, the church focuses our attention on the dignity given to the vocation of husband and father. How can St. Joseph's example of faithfulness help your family?

Prayer:

Holy Spirit, help us to set our hearts on you as Joseph did. Send your Son to live with us and to teach us. Fill us with the humility and righteousness we see in Joseph, that we would love you and embrace your will as fully as he did. Speak to us concerning our role in your plan so that we can respond to the work that you have called us to do in our homes, in the church, and in our communities.

MARCH 25

Annunciation

Solemnity

Isaiah 7:10-14
Psalm 40:7-11
Hebrews 10:4-10
Luke 1:26-38

Lo, I have I come to do thy will, O God. (Hebrews 10:7)

This refrain echoes in the hearts of all those across time who have desired to be faithful to God. In particular, it echoes Mary's "yes" as she agreed to become the mother of God, and Jesus' "yes" that he would take on human flesh from her. Their consent to the Father is a sign of the marvelous work that can be achieved even in us when we echo these words in our hearts.

Mary's "yes" to God flows from her openness to his grace. A faithful daughter of Zion, she was a member of the people God chose to be his own. In a most generous way, she heeded God's word spoken through the prophets and embraced the law he gave to guide his people. Mary had an "open ear" (Psalm 40:6), a desire to hear God and do his will. She lived what the psalmist proclaimed: "I delight to do your will, O my God; your law is within my heart" (Psalm 40:8). Because this was Mary's desire, she could say "yes" to God regardless of the unforeseen consequences.

Mary's "yes" also reflects the life she received as a member of God's chosen people. She knew that her fortunes rose and fell with those of the people God called to himself, and so she claimed as a word for herself every word God spoke to them.

On this day, when the church celebrates Mary's "yes" to God, we rejoice, for her consent brought forth God's Son who has saved the world. God's work was accomplished with Mary's cooperation because she listened to and embraced his word and because she lived as a member of the people he called to himself. Let us rejoice in Mary's "yes" and unite ourselves with her and all those throughout history who have desired to do God's will. And may these words echo in our hearts: "Here I am, Lord; I come to do your will."

Points for Meditation:

- Mary's openness to God's word and her identity with her people helped her to say "yes" to God's divine plan for humanity. What changes might be required in your own life that would help you to readily accept whatever God is calling you to do?
- The Annunciation is a feast for rejoicing. God's joy touches our lives through Mary's "yes" to him. The joy he promised to his chosen people is ours in Jesus. As you pray today, enter into this joy by thanking the Father for sending his Son to save us through his servant Mary.
- Through our baptism, we bear Christ within our hearts. He increases in us as we place our trust in him. Ask the Lord for the grace to trust him more completely so that you can make him more visible to the world.

Prayer:

Jesus, open my heart and mind so that I can trust in you completely. Like your mother Mary, give me the grace to say "yes"—without any hesitation—whenever you ask me to do your will. I rejoice in your love.

Passion (Palm) Sunday

Reading for Entrance Procession:
Cycle A: Matthew 21:1-11
Cycle B: Mark 11:1-10 or John 12:12-16
Cycle C: Luke 19:28-40

Isaiah 50:4-7
Psalm 22:8-9,17-20,23-24
Philippians 2:6-11
Cycle A: Matthew 26:14–27:66
Cycle B: Mark 14:1–15:47
Cycle C: Luke 22:14–23:56

Being found in human form he humbled himself and became obedient unto death, even death on a cross. (Philippians 2:8)

Passion Sunday marks the beginning of Holy Week. As we hold our blessed palms and proceed into the church, we can recall the perfect humility of Christ, whose triumphant entrance into Jerusalem was not in some elaborate chariot but on a simple donkey. Renouncing self-centeredness, vanity, and selfish ambition, Jesus emptied himself in order to accept his Father's will (Philippians 2:6-8).

When he became man for us, Jesus made himself poor in order that we might become rich. He took the position of a servant, even a slave, to release us from bondage to sin. He endured death so that we might live eternally with God. Jesus loved without limit. He gave himself completely to his Father and to us. Could we ever hope to attain to such love?

Mary of Bethany reflected Jesus' attitude (Mark 14:3). Moved by love for Jesus, she anointed him with a jar of precious aromatic nard. The gesture probably consumed her entire savings. Disregarding the cost, however, she poured out on Jesus everything valuable that she possessed. Her misunderstood extravagance brought ridicule from unbelieving observers (14:4-5), but her love compelled her to waste herself on Jesus—just as Jesus, out of love for the Father, "wasted" himself for us.

Mary did this because she knew how much Jesus loved her. She knew his kindness and compassion. Through his mercy, a new life had burst forth from her broken and contrite spirit. By the Holy Spirit, we too can come to know Jesus as Mary did.

On this day, we recall once again our Savior's death and resurrection. Like Mary, we too have the opportunity to anoint Jesus with our love. We too can pour out on him everything that is valuable to us—our time, our money, our energy, our life. This week, let us spread out before Jesus every other love in our lives and ask him to empower us to love him above all. Let us renounce everything that separates us from him, so that, united with him in his death, we may rise with him into new life.

Points for Meditation:

- Have you "wasted" your life on Jesus? Think of times in the past when you may have held yourself back from the Lord. Ask him for the courage to offer yourself unreservedly to him.
- Search your heart for signs of pride that keep you distant from Jesus and from others. Repent of these sins and ask Jesus to give you his humble heart.
- Meditate on the prophecy of Isaiah (50:4-7), especially the verse, "I know that I shall not be

put to shame" (50:7). How does this reflect the attitude of Jesus during his Passion?

Prayer:

Jesus, holy and anointed one, I give you all that I am and all that I have—the bad and the good. I give you my sins, my weaknesses, my loves, my possessions, my fears, my hopes. I pour out my whole life before you. Accept my love, and draw me to yourself.

EASTER TRIDUUM

Holy Thursday

Evening Mass of the Lord's Supper

Exodus 12:1-8,11-14
Psalm 116:12-13,15-18
1 Corinthians 11:23-26
John 13:1-15

As often as you eat this bread and drink the cup, you proclaim the Lord's death until he comes. (1 Corinthians 11:26)

Tonight we begin the great Easter Triduum, the commemoration of Jesus' death and resurrection. Our gathering to celebrate the Last Supper this evening is an opportunity to examine our attitude toward the Eucharist. Do we come with expectancy? Do we believe that Jesus will be present for us? Just as Jesus humbly ministered to the disciples by washing their feet, he wants to minister to us each time we celebrate the Mass.

How does Jesus want to minister to us? As he did at the Last Supper, even today, he wants to wash our feet—to cleanse us from the "dust" of walking in the world. This dust might be the guilt, fear, doubt, discouragement, illness—and much more—that accumulates and threatens to cloud our experience of the divine life that we received at baptism.

Like Peter, we too need to be clear: We do not need another bath. Nothing can undo the salvation that Jesus won for us on the cross. No sin is more powerful than Jesus. No stubbornness or hardness of heart can reverse his redemption. We do not need to be re-baptized. Still, we do need to be "dusted off" regularly so that we can continue to walk with Jesus and obey his voice.

It is essential that the lines of communication between God and ourselves be kept open, both by daily repentance and by sacramental confession, so that we can continue to grow in the love that has rescued us. As we allow Jesus to wash our feet on a regular basis, we will find ourselves living in peace and security. We will not be dismayed by the dust that clings to us so easily. We will not feel unworthy to approach the throne of God and receive his grace and mercy.

Easter draws near—the glorious celebration of Jesus' triumph over all sin and death. Throughout the Triduum, ask the Spirit to strengthen your confidence in the redemption you have received. During Mass this evening, let Jesus wash your feet and tell you, "You are clean" (John 13:10). Let him wash away the dust so that you can "go in peace to love and serve the Lord."

Points for Meditation:

- Picture in your mind the scene of Jesus washing the feet of his disciples. Now imagine yourself there in the room, while Jesus washes your feet. See him kneel down before you, washing you clean of all your sins and of all the guilt, fear, doubt, and discouragement in your life. Thank him for what he has done for you.
- During the celebration of the Eucharist, the past action of Jesus becomes present. We don't just remember the past when we participate in the Eucharistic feast—the past becomes present among us, and we are present at this saving event. While at Mass today, keep this truth in

mind, remembering that out of Christ's love for us, we receive the life of the Lord.

- If you can, after Mass, spend some time in adoration before the Blessed Sacrament tonight.

Prayer:

Thank you, Lord Jesus, for the love you poured out on the cross. You have washed us clean, and together we rejoice in the completeness of your salvation.

EASTER TRIDUUM

Good Friday

Celebration of the Lord's Passion

Isaiah 52:13–53:12
Psalm 31:2,6,12-13,15-17,25
Hebrews 4:14-16; 5:7-9
John 18:1–19:42

Upon him was the chastisement that made us whole, and with his stripes we are healed.
(Isaiah 53:5)

From a sermon by Saint Leo the Great:

True reverence for the Lord's Passion means fixing the eyes of our heart on Jesus crucified and recognizing in him our own humanity.

The earth—our earthly nature—should tremble

at the suffering of its Redeemer. The rocks—the hearts of unbelievers—should burst asunder. The dead, imprisoned in the tombs of their mortality, should come forth, the massive stones now ripped apart. Foreshadowings of the future resurrection should appear in the holy city, the Church of God: what is to happen to our bodies should now take place in our hearts.

No one, however weak, is denied a share in the victory of the cross. No one is beyond the help of the prayer of Christ. His prayer brought benefit to the multitude that raged against him. How much more does it bring to those who turn to him in repentance.

Ignorance has been destroyed, obstinacy has been overcome. The sacred blood of Christ has quenched the flaming sword that barred access to the tree of life. The age-old night of sin has given place to the true light.

The Christian people are invited to share the riches of paradise. All who have been reborn have the way open before them to return to their native land, from which they have been exiled. Unless indeed they close off for themselves the path that could be opened before the faith of a thief.

The business of this life should not preoccupy us

with its anxiety and pride, so that we no longer strive with all the love of our heart to be like our Redeemer, and to follow his example. Everything that he did or suffered was for our salvation: he wanted his body to share the goodness of its head.

First of all, in taking our human nature while remaining God, so that the Word became man, he left no member of the human race, the unbeliever excepted, without a share in his mercy. Who does not share a common nature with Christ if he has welcomed Christ, who took our nature and is reborn in the Spirit through whom Christ was conceived?

Again, who cannot recognize in Christ his own infirmities? Who would not recognize that Christ's eating and sleeping, his sadness and his shedding tears of love are marks of the nature of a slave?

It was this nature of a slave that had to be healed of its ancient wounds and cleansed of the defilement of sin. For that reason the only begotten Son of God became also the son of man. He was to have both the reality of a human nature and the fullness of the godhead.

The body that lay lifeless in the tomb is ours. The body that rose again on the third day is ours. The body that ascended above all the heights of heaven to the right hand of the Father's glory is ours. If then we walk in the way of his commandments, and are not ashamed to acknowledge the price he paid for our salvation in a lowly body, we too are to rise to share his glory. The promise he made will be fulfilled in the sight of all: Whoever acknowledges me before men, I too will acknowledge him before my Father who is in heaven.

Points for Meditation:

- Good Friday has traditionally been set aside as a day of silence. As much as you can, try to keep this silence. Spend time in quiet awe and wonder as you contemplate the Lord of all who lowered himself and took the form of a slave. Kneel in silent gratitude that you have been rescued from the sin that would have destroyed you.
- Good Friday is also a time for intercessory prayer. The liturgy includes solemn intercessions for the whole world. Ask the Lord to put on your heart someone you know and pray for that person. Pray especially for unbelievers, that the loving witness of Christians would bring them to a saving knowledge of Jesus Christ.

- If you are able, spend time with your family reading the Passion story from the Bible aloud, watching a good video of the life of Jesus, or praying the sorrowful mysteries of the rosary. Imagine yourself standing there with Jesus' followers as they watched him die on the cross.

Prayer:

Father, I worship and thank you. You gave your Son to release all humanity from sin, Satan, and death. In silent awe, I gaze upon the cross and pour out my love to you.

HOLY SATURDAY

Easter Vigil

Solemnity

Genesis 1:1–2:2
Genesis 22:1-8
Exodus 14:15–15:1
Isaiah 54:5-14
Isaiah 55:1-11
Baruch 3:9-15,32–4:4
Ezekiel 36:16-28
Romans 6:3-11
Cycle A: Matthew 28:1-10
Cycle B: Mark 16:1-8
Cycle C: Luke 24:1-12

If we have died with Christ, we believe that we shall also live with him. (Romans 6:8)

Death and life—What a stark contrast we have on this Holy Saturday! We pass through a day in the liturgy where all is silence. As the day begins, our churches will be bare—the tabernacle empty as we share liturgically in Jesus' death and burial. Yet, as the Easter Vigil begins this evening, we will be introduced once again into the fullness of life through his resurrection to glory. Tonight, our churches will be resplendent with new life and beauty. The contrast in the course of a single day couldn't be any greater.

In a passage that is always read at the Easter Vigil, St. Paul teaches us that we share both in Jesus' death and in his resurrection (Romans 6:3-11). Our own baptism is itself a paradox of life and death. Through baptism into Jesus' death on the cross, we die to sin. And, through the same baptism into his resurrection, we too are raised to a new life in his Spirit. What a glorious contrast our life is meant to be! As we die every day to self and sin, we receive new life through the power of Jesus' resurrection. The life of the risen Lord is in us because we have been baptized into him. His power is within us to change us. By his Spirit, we can begin to live a new life.

Holy Saturday gives us an opportunity to seek this new life by spending time in prayer and reading God's word. As much as we are able, let us make this a day of seeking God in eager watching and waiting.

Let us anticipate the gift of new life that we will receive tonight as we renew our baptismal vows and participate in the Easter liturgy.

Today we can grow closer to Jesus and receive more of his life. Jesus has conquered sin, death, and Satan. We can experience the victory of his death and resurrection this day. We can expect tangible changes in our lives in the days and weeks ahead, because we have received the power of the risen Jesus.

Points for Meditation:

- Think over the past year. In what ways have you "died" with Jesus to sin, self-love, and self-centeredness? Ask Jesus to give you a greater faith to believe that when you unite yourself with him, the power sin has over you can be broken even more.
- Even if you don't attend an Easter Vigil Mass, read through the seven Old Testament readings that are part of the liturgy for this day. Take special note of how God worked throughout history to form his people and save them from sin. Offer praise to the Father for the new covenant he has given you through his Son Jesus.

Tonight all those who have been preparing to enter the church will be baptized. Intercede for them, especially any candidates who will be baptized in your parish. Pray that the Father would pour out his Spirit upon them in a mighty way.

Prayer:

Jesus, I want to share more deeply in your life this day. Help me to overcome sin through the power of your death and resurrection. Give me, and all those who enter the church today, new life in the Holy Spirit!

EASTER SUNDAY

Resurrection of the Lord

Solemnity

Acts 10:34,37-43
Psalm 118:1-2,16-17,22-23
Colossians 3:1-4 or 1 Corinthians 5:6-8
John 20:1-9

Then the other disciple, who reached the tomb first, also went in, and he saw and believed. (John 20:8)

The gospel reading from John may seem odd, because we hear only part of the story of the resurrection. Neither Mary Magdalene or the disciples encounter the risen Lord. Yet such a reading can bring their experience closer to ours. During the course of this Passover weekend, the disciples' faith was stretched greatly. Until they encountered the risen Christ, they could only hope and trust in his promise that he would rise.

Similarly, we ourselves have not encountered the risen Christ in the flesh. So this is a time of faith for us as well. Yet, unlike these first disciples, we do not have to wait with anxiety and fear. We have the Holy Spirit living in us to give us confidence that the resurrection is real. Our faith in Jesus Christ, risen from the dead, comes from the Spirit. It is he who convinces us of realities that we will not see until the final day of the Lord.

That's why Easter is such a day of celebration: The Holy Spirit is making Jesus' resurrection real to us! He wants to bring us the freedom from sin that Jesus accomplished on the cross. We are no longer slaves to sin. We don't have to see Jesus with our eyes; we can receive him in our hearts! Even death cannot overcome us!

We have the opportunity today to go beyond an intellectual faith to a faith that is living in our hearts. Christ is risen! He has cleansed us of every sin. We will not die; we will live with him forever! If you have not experienced this indescribable joy, today is the day to start. The Holy Spirit is ready to show you the love and power of God. Today is the day to experience these glorious truths in a way that will cause you to shout aloud: "He is risen!" The words will ring with meaning for you if you ask the Spirit to reveal them to your heart.

Points for Meditation:

- In prayer, ask the Lord to show you how the resurrection of his Son can affect you in a tangible way. In what ways can the risen Christ be manifested in you and through you?
- Whatever trials or struggles you may be experiencing in your life right now, ask the Holy Spirit to give you a deep sense of joy today, especially as you receive the body and blood of Jesus in the Eucharist.
- Spend some time meditating on these words of St. Anselm: "You were a bond-slave and by this man you are free. By him you are brought back from exile; lost, you are restored; dead, you are raised."

Prayer:

Jesus, what words of praise can I offer you? Death has been swallowed up in your victory. Your divine life is now alive within me. Lord Jesus, I will love and praise you forever!

APRIL 25

St. Mark, evangelist

Feast

1 Peter 5:5-14
Psalm 89:2-3,6-7,16-17
Mark 16:15-20

Cast all your anxieties on him, for he cares about you. (1 Peter 5:7)

Such words of comfort, attributed to the apostle Peter, reflect a deep knowledge of Jesus' love, and they fittingly commemorate the feast of St. Mark. Ancient tradition describes Mark as Peter's assistant—his "son" in faith (1 Peter 5:13). So it's not surprising that the passage from the first Letter of Peter reveals the same sense of personal experience and complete trust in God that is portrayed throughout the Gospel of Mark.

According to tradition, Mark accompanied Paul and Barnabas on some of their missionary journeys (Acts 12:25). Despite a falling out with Paul (which seemingly saw eventual reconciliation), Mark continued to labor for the early church and went on to serve in Rome with Peter. Later, either under Peter's instructions in Rome or on his own as a pastor in Alexandria, Mark is thought to have authored his gospel for the Roman Christians suffering persecution under Nero in the late 60s A.D.

The Gospel of Mark reveals an author who exemplified the very traits extolled in Peter's exhortation. Mark taught that true discipleship meant following the humble example of Jesus who "came not to be served but to serve" (Mark 10:45). Mark echoed this call throughout his gospel. His narrative gives us a glimpse through his personal experience of how much the Lord cares for us.

The love of God revealed in Mark's inspired words gave hope to the early community of believers, even though many of them were eventually martyred. By word and example, Mark has taught generations of disciples to trust the Lord completely by taking up his cross and following him (Mark 8:34). We too can experience God's ability to restore, establish, and strengthen us as we turn to him each day (1 Peter 5:10). This is something Peter and Mark both experienced, and something that is available to us as well. Let us humble ourselves so that we too can experience our Father's love.

Points for Meditation:

- St. Mark lived and wrote in turbulent times. If you were a Christian in Rome during Nero's persecution, what would you have found most encouraging about the gospel that Mark wrote?
- One of the last instructions of Jesus in Mark's Gospel is to "Go into all the world and preach the gospel to the whole creation" (Mark 16:15). On this feast of St. Mark, take time to examine how you can proclaim the good news more fully in your home and where you work.
- As he lived out his evangelistic vocation, St. Mark must have had plenty of occasions to "cast his anxieties" (1 Peter 5:7) on the Lord. Pray about one anxiety that you are holding onto. Place it at the feet of the Lord and surrender your cares to him.

Prayer:

We praise you, Lord, and place our lives in your care. Teach us to trust in you and to be watchful against the prowling of the devil.

MAY 3

Sts. Philip and James, apostles

Feast

1 Corinthians 15:1-8
Psalm 19:2-5
John 14:6-14

Truly, truly, I say to you, he who believes in me will also do the works that I do. (John 14:12)

The apostles Philip and James are honored on the same feast day because their relics are contained under the main altar of the Church of the Twelve Apostles in Rome, which was dedicated on May 3 in the year 565. According to the Gospel of John, Philip came from Bethsaida off the shore of the Lake of Galilee (John 1:44). He may have been a friend or business partner of Andrew and Peter, who also came from that city. James, the son of Alphaeus, is called the "younger" or "lesser" to distinguish him from the better-known James, the brother of John.

He may have been a relative of Jesus, and the same James who led the early Jerusalem community (Acts 15; Galatians 1:19; 2:9) and who wrote the New Testament Letter of James.

In the Acts of the Apostles, we see how Philip and James and all the other apostles were able to preach boldly about Jesus, perform miracles, and advance the kingdom of God on earth with great enthusiasm and dedication. What turned Philip, James, and these other ordinary men into strong people capable of withstanding persecution and suffering as they brought the message of Jesus to the world? Part of the answer lies in the reading from the Gospel of John.

Jesus was surprised when Philip asked him to show them the Father (John 14:8). Didn't Philip realize that Jesus could only do what he did and love as he loved by the power of God? No mere mortal could have power over sickness and death, or the patience, love, and compassion of Jesus, if he were not one with the Father. Much of Jesus' teaching centers around this one astounding truth—that he and the Father are one.

Jesus issued a challenge to the apostles when he said that if they believed in him, they would also do the works that he did—and even greater works. The challenge was to rise above human limitations through their faith in the indwelling power of God. This is the very same challenge that Jesus gives to us. Just as the Spirit descended upon the apostles at Pentecost and filled them with the presence of Christ, the same Spirit now comes upon us in baptism and fills us! No obstacle is too big, no weakness too daunting. We can do all things through Christ who strengthens us (Philippians 4:13).

Jesus promised that he would never abandon us or leave us orphaned. He has been true to his word. Let us ask for a greater outpouring of the Holy Spirit upon us and for a greater realization of the presence of Christ within us. We may be ordinary people, but with Christ we can become extraordinary vessels of the love of God in this world.

Points for Meditation:

- Like Philip, we all long to know God. In every person's heart is the same prayer: "Show us the Father, and we shall be satisfied" (John 14:8). Reflect on the truth that in Jesus, the immense gap between God and ourselves is bridged.

- Think of one situation or area in your life where you feel weak or stretched beyond your capacity. Then meditate on Philippians 4:13: "I can do all things in him who strengthens me." Ask God to strengthen your faith in his presence within you to overcome all obstacles.
- After encountering the risen Christ (1 Corinthians 15:7), Philip and James were compelled to preach the message of salvation so that others might know the joy of their redemption. Ask the Holy Spirit to give you a firm and secure grasp of the gospel so that you are able to witness to others about God's love and mercy as shown through Jesus Christ.

Prayer:

Jesus, you sent the Holy Spirit to dwell in us, to guide us, and to empower us to be your witnesses. Your presence is our comfort and consolation, our inspiration and power. We love you and want to be with you always.

MAY 14

St. Matthias, apostle

Feast

Acts 1:15-17,20-26
Psalm 113:1-8
John 15:9-17

You did not choose me, but I chose you and appointed you that you should go and bear fruit and that your fruit should abide.
(John 15:16)

Jesus' words, addressed to his apostles, are for all of us. We are called to be disciples—to follow and learn from him how to bear much fruit and how to love one another. The call flows from the Father's love for us, and can only be answered as we abide in that love (John 15:9)—continuing in it, holding to it, defending it, suffering the consequences of it. We remain in it as we obey his command, "Love one another as I have loved you," learning from the

Father as Jesus did (15:12,15). We can only love one another as we experience God's love for us, learning from him what it means to be loved.

We learn by abiding in Christ—especially by defending our minds against the lies that confront us daily. Our experiences in the world seek to contradict the truth that God loves and cares for us and has all the power necessary to keep us at the center of his will. Yet the truth remains that we have been chosen by Christ, designated as disciples, to go and bear fruit that will last. We can bear no lasting fruit, be no true disciples, unless we abide in him (John 15:4,8).

St. Matthias can be a model for us. Not much is known about him, except that he was chosen to replace Judas Iscariot who betrayed Jesus (Acts 1:15-26). Matthias adhered to Jesus' teaching and continued in it, bearing fruit for God, even though it has remained largely "hidden" fruit. As a hidden disciple—that is, one about whom little is known—he points the way for us, most of whom live hidden lives. As we respond to Jesus' call to be disciples, as we abide in God's love and learn from him what love is and how to love each other, we will bear fruit in our families and work, even though it might not attract much attention.

Jesus has chosen us—to love in the circumstances of our lives and to bear fruit for him.

Points for Meditation:

- Examine your relationship with God and with those people who are closest to you. Do they show evidence of bearing "fruit"? Pray about how you can make them even more fruitful.
- Jesus told his apostles that they had been "chosen" by him. Matthias was chosen by God to be the twelfth apostle to replace Judas Iscariot. How does the realization that you are "chosen" by God change the way you view your service to the Lord? How does it change the way you look at the events in your life and the place where the Lord has you now?
- Instead of choosing on their own who was to become the twelfth apostle, Peter and the other apostles prayed for discernment, knowing that only God could read the hearts of men (Acts 1:24). Recall a time in the past when you sought the Lord's guidance by praying about an upcoming decision. Are there any impending decisions in your life you could pray about and seek the Lord's will before taking action?

Prayer:

Holy Spirit, teacher and guide, lead us in the calling we have received, even to be hidden disciples of Jesus. Open our hearts to abide in the Father's love. As we learn of his unfathomable love for us, help us to love one another with the same love.

Ascension of Our Lord

Solemnity

(Celebrated the Thursday following the sixth Sunday of Easter)

Acts 1:1-11
Psalm 47:2-3,6-9
Ephesians 1:17-23
Cycle A: Matthew 28:16-20
Cycle B: Mark 16:15-20
Cycle C: Luke 24:46-53

May you know what is the hope to which he has called you, what are the riches of his glorious inheritance in the saints, and what is the immeasurable greatness of his power in us who believe. (Ephesians 1:18-19)

On the feast of the Ascension, we are called to rejoice, both in Jesus' victory over sin and death, and in the glorious life that he has secured for us. We pray that we would know three specific aspects of the new life that is ours in Christ: "the hope to which he has called" us, "his glorious inheritance in the saints," and "the immeasurable greatness of his power in us who believe."

As Christians, our hope is secure because it rests in Jesus' death and resurrection. Because Jesus has overcome sin forever, we can live in freedom and peace, no matter what situations we may face. We have been reconciled to God. We are no longer strangers. Every day, we can live in confidence, knowing that our God is with us to strengthen and comfort us.

Our hope is also founded in the inheritance Jesus won for us—none other than being with our Father forever, knowing him intimately, in all his splendor and beauty. In his ascension, Jesus has opened the door for us. Though we are sinners, we have been forgiven and redeemed. We are now fully loved and accepted as God's children, and we will live with him forever.

As we live every day in the hope of our eternal inheritance, however, we can begin to taste these blessings here and now. This is part of the "immeasurable greatness of his power in us who believe." Before he returned to his Father, Jesus promised his disciples that anyone who believed in him would be able to cast out demons, heal the sick, and perform signs and wonders in his name (Mark 16:17-18). How? By the power of the Holy Spirit, who lives inside of us. The same Spirit who raised Jesus from the dead is in our hearts, inviting us to yield to him and empowering us to live in the victory of the resurrection. No challenge is too great for a child of God!

Points for Meditation:

- As the disciples watched Jesus being lifted up to heaven, do you think that they would have been tempted to feel abandoned and panicked about their risen Lord leaving the earth? Think of a time in your life when you felt as if Jesus had abandoned you. How can Jesus' promise of the Holy Spirit (Acts 1:5,8) bring you comfort at such a time?
- Exercise your hope today by calling to mind Jesus' death and resurrection and the salvation he won for you on the cross. How can you more fully place your hope and confidence in these truths?
- Have you "tasted" the blessings here and now of your eternal inheritance? Ask God for a powerful

outpouring of his Spirit on you, so that he can manifest his power in your life.

Prayer:

Lord Jesus, we rejoice today in your ascension to the Father's right hand. Thank you, Lord, for offering us a share in your heavenly life. By your Spirit, help us to lay hold of our inheritance in you—the hope, the glory, and the power that are the right of every child of God.

MAY 31

Visitation of Mary

Feast

Zephaniah 3:14-18 or Romans 12:9-16
(Psalm) Isaiah 12:2-6
Luke 1:39-56

Sing aloud, O daughter of Zion; shout, O Israel! Rejoice and exult with all your heart, O daughter of Jerusalem! (Zephaniah 3:14)

A sense of joy fills the church today as we celebrate the visitation of Mary to her cousin Elizabeth. This joy is not just because Mary showed deep charity to Elizabeth by traveling to help her during her pregnancy, even though she herself was with child. It is not only that Elizabeth, who was unable to conceive a child, was now anticipating an event long thought impossible. Nor is it that all humanity would know good fortune through the children these women were carrying in their wombs.

The joy encompasses all these, but is far greater still. The church rejoices because, through Mary, we can see God's hand touching his beloved people, bringing from among them the one who would bring salvation to the whole world. It is no wonder that this is a day of rejoicing, for in Jesus we see the fulfillment of the prophet's words: "The king of Israel, the Lord, is in your midst; you shall fear evil no more" (Zephaniah 3:15). In Mary's womb was the one who most perfectly fulfilled these prophetic words.

As part of God's announcement to Mary that she would conceive and bear a child (Luke 1:31,43), he gave a sign. Elizabeth, "who was called barren," had conceived (Luke 1:36). Both the virgin Mary and the barren Elizabeth had conceived through the intervention of God. In this, they joined those childless women of the Old Testament who were similarly blessed by God: Sarah (Genesis 18:9-15); Rebekah (Genesis 25:21-22); Rachel (Genesis 29:31, 30:22-24); and Hannah (1 Samuel 1:11,19-20). God's blessing on all these women was for a specific purpose in salvation history.

And so it was with Mary: She was blessed by God by becoming, in her virginity, the mother of the Savior.

In the visitation, we see a striking parallel between Elizabeth and Mary: God worked in a marvelous and sovereign way in bringing life into the wombs of women for whom it was humanly impossible. But since with God nothing is impossible (Luke 1:37), the miracle is itself a sign that the life Jesus brings is not of human origin or conception.

In Mary, God's long preparation for the salvation of his people advanced. A Savior would come, and daughter Jerusalem could rejoice. Let us join in this gladness, for from this ancient people has come the Savior of the world.

Points for Meditation:

- Pray through today's responsorial from Isaiah 12:2-6. As you do, let the prophet's words reflect the joy and gratitude in your heart for the glorious things God has done through Jesus.
- When Elizabeth saw Mary, she exclaimed, "Blessed is she who believed that there would be a fulfillment of what was spoken to her from the Lord" (Luke 1:45). What promises do you think God will fulfill in your life? How can your faith in God's promises bring blessings to you?

How did the time that Mary and Elizabeth spent together help prepare them for their role in salvation history? Is there someone in your life whom you could support—through time spent together and through service—to help prepare them to fulfill the mission God has given to them?

Prayer:

Holy Spirit, thank you for inspiring Mary to visit Elizabeth. Keep us open to your inspirations as well, so that we may be instruments of your grace wherever you call us to be of service.

PENTECOST SUNDAY

Solemnity

(Celebrated on the seventh Sunday after Easter)

Vigil:
Genesis:11:1-9 or Exodus 19:2-8,16-20 or Ezekiel 37:1-14 or Joel 3:1-5
Psalm 104:1-2,24,27-30,35
Romans 8:22-27
John 7:37-39

Mass During the Day:
Acts 2:1-11
Psalm 104:1,24,29-31,34
1 Corinthians 12:3-7,12-13
John 20:19-23

And there appeared to them tongues as of fire, distributed and resting on each one of them. (Acts 2:3)

The feast of Pentecost is one of the most powerful reminders to us that God's intentions go far beyond forgiveness. He wants us to participate in the life of Christ and become living witnesses to that life for everyone we meet. Every Christian is meant to be a living sign that Jesus Christ has conquered sin and now reigns as Lord over all.

Do you believe that in Christ, by the power of his Spirit, you are a new creation? During Jesus' earthly life, the Holy Spirit had not yet been poured out on all people (John 7:39). It was on the cross that Jesus delivered his Spirit to the Father (Luke 23:45) and to us (John 19:30). And, it is at baptism that we die with Jesus so that "we too might walk in newness of life" (Romans 6:4).

On Easter Sunday, Jesus breathed the Spirit on his disciples, re-creating them as fully as when his Father breathed life into our first parents (John 20:22; Genesis 2:7). By the power of the Spirit, each of us now has a new beginning, a way out of every form of sin and bondage. The Spirit has come to give us a new dignity as beloved children of God. He has come to transform us to such a degree that we actually take on the personality of Christ.

Jesus was "the grain of wheat" that had to die in order to bear "much fruit" (John 12:24). This grain, planted on Good Friday, has borne a mighty harvest, a re-created humanity that thinks, loves, and chooses in union with Almighty God. Each of us is called to be a part of this new humanity by welcoming the Spirit into our daily lives. This is the only way that we will become as Christ to this world.

It is the role of the Spirit to bring us to a daily, personal encounter with Jesus. He wants to look into our souls, judge all that is light and dark within us, forgive us, heal us, and call us "beloved." When the Spirit is at work in us, the Scriptures come alive. They pierce us with the overwhelming love of God and fill us with a desire to pour out our lives to him. This is the one foundation that will enable us to touch the throne of God in our prayer and live a life of faith in this fallen world.

Today, and every day, the Holy Spirit wants to reveal Jesus' majesty to our innermost being. He wants to show us that Jesus is the Savior from sin and death, the victor over the evil one, the Lord of all. When we experience Jesus in such an intimate, powerful way, we are moved to surrender our own ways, our own wisdom, and our own desires to him.

By the Spirit, God wants to give us the grace to understand his will, to choose his will, and to do his will. The same Spirit who empowered Peter to proclaim the resurrection of Christ with such boldness, the same Spirit who gave Paul the courage and persistence to preach throughout the Roman empire, the same Spirit who sustained Mary every day of her life—this Spirit wants to work in us just as powerfully.

On this great feast day, drink deeply of the Spirit. Don't just ask for a sip, as if that's all you deserve. Don't seek only to quench your thirst so that you can go back to living as you used to. Don't sell the Spirit short. Ask for a fountain of the Spirit inside of you—a fountain of living water that fills you to overflowing, saturates your heart with the love of the Father, and flows out to everyone you meet.

Points for Meditation:

- Think over the past year since last Pentecost. Recount specific instances where the Spirit moved you to act differently than you would have done otherwise.
- Meditate on the gifts of the Holy Spirit listed in Isaiah 11:2 and in 1 Corinthians 12. Ask the

Lord which gift he might want to manifest in you in a greater way this year.

- Pentecost is a great day to ask for a renewed outpouring of the Holy Spirit. If you are able, gather together with several Christian friends and pray with each other for the renewal of the Holy Spirit's action in your life.

Prayer:

Father, pour the living water of the Holy Spirit over my heart so that I might bear fruit for you. Come, Holy Spirit, and reveal Jesus to my heart today. Let me know the Lord and the power of his resurrection. I want to become a new creation today.

TRINITY SUNDAY

Solemnity

(Celebrated on the Sunday after Pentecost)

Cycle A: Exodus 34:4-6,8-9
(Psalm) Daniel 3:52-56
2 Corinthians 13:11-13
John 3:16-18

Cycle B: Deuteronomy 4:32-34,39-40
Psalm 33:4-6,9,18-20,22
Romans 8:14-17
Matthew 28:16-20

Cycle C: Proverbs 8:22-31
Psalm 8:4-9
Romans 5:1-5
John 16:12-15

God so loved the world that he gave his only Son, that whoever believes in him should not perish but have eternal life. (John 3:16)

"In the name of the Father, and of the Son, and of the Holy Spirit."

Every time we bless ourselves, we proclaim the mystery of the Trinity. Only the Christian religion teaches that there are three Persons in one God. It is a mystery we will never be able to fully comprehend. Yet it is the heart and soul of our Christian life.

St. Ignatius of Loyola once had a revelation of the Trinity as a harmonic chord, with three notes being played at the same time but forming one sound. This revelation was so overwhelming that after receiving it, he wept tears of joy all day. God is not an isolated, contained being. His nature is to be communal. The one being of God is really the interrelationship between the Father, the Son, and the Holy Spirit.

As Christians, we share in this Trinitarian love and life. God is not some impersonal force living far away from us in some other universe. He sent his Son to become one of us so that we could share in his eternal and all-consuming personal life. As disciples of Jesus, we are invited to live within the love of the Holy Trinity. At baptism, we received the intimate, divine life of the Father, Son, and Holy

Spirit. Through the death and resurrection of Jesus, we become sons and daughters of the Father. By the power of the Holy Spirit, he is our Father, just as Jesus is our brother.

We should never view the Trinity as only an intellectual concept that has no practical bearing on our lives. The Trinity is our life. Every day we can affirm this truth. We live within the love offered to us each moment by a merciful God who wants us within the very center of his being. To gain us this privilege, the Father sacrificed his Son on the cross. The Holy Spirit has been given to us as a foretaste of the heavenly joys that await us. On this feast day of the Trinity, let us rejoice at the gift of life and love that has been so freely offered.

Points for Meditation:

- Spend time today praying to each Person of the Trinity. Thank the Father, your Creator, for the magnificence of the earth and for the life he has given to you. Thank the Son, Jesus Christ, for his obedience to his Father's will and for the shedding of his blood, which has redeemed you. Thank the Holy Spirit, who sanctifies you by his presence and who inflames your heart with love for God.

- Meditate on John 3:16. Renounce any thoughts you might have that you are not worthy of God's love. In your mind, reaffirm the truth that God loves you passionately and unconditionally, and that he wants to share his life with you.
- As you contemplate the love in the Trinity, ask the Holy Spirit to show you where you need to love others the way God loves you. Then ask him for the grace to do so.

Prayer:

God, we praise you: Father all-powerful, Christ Lord and Savior, Spirit of love. You reveal yourself in the depths of our being, drawing us to share in your life and your love. One God, three Persons, be near to the people formed in your image, close to the world your love brings to life. (*Alternative Opening Prayer for Trinity Sunday*)

Corpus Christi Sunday

Solemnity

(Celebrated on the Sunday after Trinity Sunday)

Cycle A: Deuteronomy 8:2-3,14-16
Psalm 147:12-15,19-20
1 Corinthians 10:16-17
John 6:51-58

Cycle B: Exodus 24:3-8
Psalm 116:12-13,15-18
Hebrews 9:11-15
Mark 14:12-16,22-26

Cycle C: Genesis 14:18-20
Psalm 110:1-4
1 Corinthians 11:23-26
Luke 9:11-17

I am the living bread which came down from heaven. (John 6:51)

The feast of Corpus Christi celebrates the very heart of our lives as children of God: our new covenant in Jesus' blood. Because Jesus offered himself for our sins, we can now be reconciled with our Father in heaven and receive his life. This is the covenant we celebrate every time we gather to receive Jesus' body and blood in the Eucharist.

For thousands of years, the people of the Old Testament equated blood with life. On Mount Sinai, Moses ratified the Israelites' covenant with Yahweh by sprinkling the sacrificial blood of a bull on the people and the altar (Exodus 24:3-8). The people accepted Yahweh as their God, and their relationship with him was sealed in blood. They were joined in a bond of life.

In a similar—but far more powerful—way, Jesus established our new covenant by offering his own blood as a sacrifice of atonement for our sin (Hebrews 9:11-15). The blood of bulls and rams was no longer sufficient. Only the life-blood of the eternal Son of God made flesh could bring about the relationship God longed to have with his people.

This is the wonder of the gift of Jesus' body and blood in the Eucharist. No longer do we simply agree to live by the law of God; we embrace the Lord himself, eating his body and drinking his blood. We are no longer sprinkled clean by an external washing. Instead, we allow Jesus into our hearts and ask him to live within us, transforming us into his image.

This is the covenant God had long desired to establish with his people. Through the prophet Jeremiah, he promised that he would place his law deep within our hearts (Jeremiah 31:31-34). Now, though the sacrifice of Jesus' body and blood, we can be drawn into a relationship with God so intimate that we begin to take on his characteristics. His love, his compassion, and his desires become our own.

Points for Meditation:

- Jesus fed the crowd of five thousand because he did not want them to go away hungry. In the same way, he satisfies our hunger for him through his body and blood. Think of the hunger you have for Christ in your life. As you receive the Eucharist today, recall that Jesus' body and blood can satisfy your deepest desires.
- Jesus gave himself to us under the form of bread and wine so that he could be sacramentally present to us always. Meditate on the truth that Jesus wants so intimate a union with you that he

offers you his own flesh and blood. Pray over the Scripture verse: "He who eats my flesh and drinks my blood abides in me, and I in him" (John 6:56).

- Make an effort to receive the Eucharist during the week, or spend time in prayer before the Blessed Sacrament. Praise and thank the Father for giving us his Son in the new covenant of Jesus' blood.

Prayer:

Father, every time we receive Jesus' body and blood with grateful and humble hearts, we ask you to enter more deeply into our lives. By your Spirit, reveal to us the promises that are ours through this new covenant.

SACRED HEART OF JESUS

Solemnity

(Celebrated on the Friday after Corpus Christi Sunday)

Cycle A: Deuteronomy 7:6-11
Psalm 103:1-4,6-8,10
1 John 4:7-16
Matthew 11:25-30

Cycle B: Hosea 11:1,3-4,8-9
(Psalm) Isaiah 12:2-6
Ephesians 3:8-12,14-19
John 19:31-37

Cycle C: Ezekiel 34:11-16
Psalm 23:1-6
Romans 5:5-11
Luke 15:3-7

Behold, I, I myself will search for my sheep, and will seek them out. (Ezekiel 34:11)

Father, you have loved us as your own children. From age to age you have shown us compassion and love, and in the fullness of time you acted to take away our burdens and meet all our needs. All praise to you Father, that from your heart of love, you give us the sacred heart of your Son, Jesus.

From all eternity, your heart beats with love for each one of us. Though we have sinned against you again and again, you would not treat us as our sins deserved. All praise to you, Father, that you allowed the heart of your precious Son to be pierced for us. Because of him, we are free!

Jesus, your sacred heart is the source and ocean of infinite mercy. All praise to you, Lord, that even in our sinfulness, we are washed clean in this limitless ocean. Your sacred heart is the propitiation for our sins. Because you were obedient, even unto death, your heart was bruised for our offenses and pierced for our iniquities. All praise to you, Lord, for your heart is the salvation of all who trust in you.

Jesus, your heart burns with charity and generosity toward us. It is full of goodness and kindness for us, infinitely patient with our weaknesses. All praise to you, Lord, for you will never turn us away.

Jesus, in your heart we find all wisdom and knowledge. We find all peace, compassion, and consolation. All praise to you, Lord, that every moment of every day, we can turn to your heart and find our refuge.

Jesus, you love us so deeply that after you died on the cross for us, you did not leave us abandoned. You sent your Holy Spirit to dwell in our hearts and promised that you will come back to us, to take us to be with you forever. Lord, we thank you that you are so deeply in love with us that you never want to be separated from us.

Points for Meditation:

- In the 1670s, St. Margaret Mary Alacoque, a French nun, received visions of Jesus in which he asked to be honored under the symbol of his heart. In one vision, Margaret Mary rested her head upon Jesus' heart, while he disclosed the wonders of his love for mankind. In prayer, imagine yourself laying your head on the heart of Jesus. What would he say to you?
- Read Ezekiel 34:11-16 in light of what God has done for us through Jesus. Through his death and resurrection, Jesus has gathered us from the

countries of the world and joined us to faithful Israel (Ezekiel 34:13). We are blessed with good pasture (34:14) in Jesus, both by his words and by his body in the Eucharist. He will take care of everyone (34:16) personally, for he is the Good Shepherd (34:15). Has there ever been a time in your life when Jesus sought you out or rescued you? Praise God for his faithfulness.

- Jesus' heart is an ocean of mercy. Intercede for men and women everywhere, that they would come to know the compassionate and gentle heart of their Savior.

Prayer:

Holy Spirit, you are the comforter of all people. In your mercy, call us back to the heart of our Lord, the source of all comfort. Lead us each day into the sacred heart of Jesus, where we can find rest from all our weariness and burdens. May we lose ourselves in the endless mercy of his heart!

IMMACULATE HEART OF MARY

Memorial

(Celebrated on the Saturday after the Sacred Heart of Jesus)

Luke 2:41-51

[Jesus] went down with them and came to Nazareth, and was obedient to them; and his mother kept all these things in her heart. (Luke 2:51)

As we celebrate the feast of the Immaculate Heart of Mary, we can reflect on Mary's witness and on the example it sets for all believers. While Mary was the mother of the Redeemer, she was also dependent—like the rest of us—on the Redeemer's saving grace. We may not be sinless like she was; nevertheless, we are called to live the life of the new creation that Mary so perfectly embodied.

"If anyone is in Christ, he is a new creation; the old has passed away, behold, the new has come" (2 Corinthians 5:17). Mary's heart was set on pleasing God. In everything she did, she demonstrated a childlike faith and trust in God and his promises to her. When she accepted the angel's call to be the mother of the Messiah, Mary freely surrendered her rights to a "normal" life. Instead, she determined to follow God's plan—wherever it led. All of us who have experienced the love and forgiveness of God in a personal way understand how dramatically our entire perspective can be changed by one touch from the Lord.

"[Jesus] died for all, that those who live might live no longer for themselves but for him who for their sake died and was raised" (2 Corinthians 5:15). As a new creation living for Jesus, our lives should be drastically different from those whose hearts are set on this world alone. When we live for Jesus, we no longer live for ourselves or for the approval of others, but to please the one who died for us! Because of his love, we find ourselves compelled to love in return. We want to become ambassadors for Christ, bringing his life and light to a world in desperate need.

Mary's entire life was set on fulfilling God's plan and advancing his kingdom. In prayer, she sought out his wisdom and direction and then moved in simple, trusting obedience. Neither years of patient waiting nor the painful culmination of Jesus' ministry caused her to lose heart. Let us imitate Mary's example: By faith, she moved in the freedom of a true daughter of God.

Points for Meditation:

- As you continue to deepen your commitment to Jesus, how has your perspective changed? Do you find yourself becoming less attached to material things? Do you find yourself thinking more about the Lord as you go about your day? Think of all the ways in which your goals and ambitions have changed since you accepted Jesus into your life in a deeper way.
- This feast came about as the culmination of a devotion—which arose in the seventeenth century—to Mary's immaculate heart. The day for the feast was set for the day after the Sacred Heart of Jesus because Mary's heart is such a clear reflection of the heart of her son. Today is a good time to look into your own heart. Is it a reflection of the heart of Jesus? Repent of anything that might be locked away in your heart that would keep you separated from your Lord and Savior.

In what ways do you think Mary experienced freedom as a result of her simple trust and obedience? Think of areas in your life where a greater level of trust and obedience would help to free you from doubts and anxieties. Then surrender these areas over to God. Tell him you will trust in his plan for your life.

Prayer:

Lord Jesus, thank you for the example of the new creation we find in Mary, your mother. Grant us pure hearts like hers so that we might better imitate her faith and obedience.

JUNE 11

St. Barnabas, apostle

Memorial

Acts 11:21-26; 13:1-3
Psalm 98:1-6
Matthew 10:7-13

He was a good man, full of the Holy Spirit and of faith. (Acts 11:24)

Everyone would like to have a friend like Barnabas. He demonstrated so many impressive and endearing qualities that we feel ourselves drawn to him. Born of a Levite family on the island of Cyprus, Barnabas was sent to Jerusalem for his education, where he became a disciple of Jesus. So touching was this man's witness to Christ that in addition to his given name of Joseph, the apostles nicknamed him Barnabas—"son of consolation" or "son of encouragement" (Acts 4:36)—a name that stayed with him all his life.

Throughout his Christian life, Barnabas showed the heart of a true disciple of Jesus, demonstrating the characteristics that Jesus taught his first followers (Matthew 10:1-42). His primary instruction was that they preach the gospel, raise the dead, cast out demons, and heal the sick (10:8). Above anything else, they were sent out to advance the kingdom of God by the power of the Spirit. Barnabas showed this single-mindedness when he went to Antioch to care for the newly-converted Gentiles there (Acts 11:22) as well as when he introduced Saul, the persecutor-turned-believer, to the apostles in Jerusalem (9:27).

In both instances, Barnabas revealed an openness to the Holy Spirit that led him into new and uncomfortable situations with confidence and peace. Barnabas understood that disciples of Jesus were not to concern themselves primarily with their own circumstances or with other people's expectations. Rather, their confidence and security were to come from knowing God's call and trusting in his provision. Barnabas stood by Paul at a critical moment, when no one else was willing to support him. Furthermore, he was open to allowing the Gentiles to accept Christ without submitting to the entire Mosaic law. This would not have been easy, but because of Barnabas' work, the church was able to grow both in numbers and in maturity.

We can know the same power and authority that Barnabas and all the other apostles knew. Jesus has given his Holy Spirit to each of us, and he has called each of us into his service. As we allow Jesus' presence to increase in us, we give God the freedom to work through us, advancing his kingdom on the earth.

Points for Meditation:

- Think of the spiritual gifts that might help you to step out boldly in faith in situations when you feel out of your "comfort zone." Pray to the Lord for an outpouring of these gifts in your life.
- Barnabas received his new name because of his generous acts of consolation and encouragement. How often do you encourage or console your spouse, children, and friends? What changes in your attitude would help you become a person who—even without consciously thinking about it beforehand—seeks to encourage his brothers and sisters in Christ?
- Barnabas was able to recognize the genuine grace of conversion in Saul and courageously

befriend him. Do we set up impossible standards for others before we are willing to grant them our acceptance? Ask the Lord to banish any attitudes of prejudice and judgmentalism that you might be harboring.

Prayer:

Heavenly Father, help us to be like St. Barnabas in humbly responding to your Spirit. We give you permission to move freely in us for the glory of your name and the growth of the church.

JUNE 24

Birth of St. John the Baptist

Solemnity

Vigil:
Jeremiah 1:4-10
Psalm 71:1-6,15,17
1 Peter 1:8-12
Luke 1:5-17

Mass during the Day:
Isaiah 49:1-6
Psalm 139:1-3,13-15
Acts 13:22-26
Luke 1:57-66,80

Do not be afraid, Zechariah, for your prayer is heard, and your wife Elizabeth will bear you a son, and you shall call his name John. (Luke 1:13)

Zechariah and Elizabeth wanted so much to have a child, especially as they watched their neighbors' families grow. But as deep as their desire was, deeper still was God's desire that their faith in him grow. This was, in part, the fruit of their long years of waiting for the Lord to fulfill their dreams. Day by day, as they prayed for a child, they were challenged to continue to hope in God. Every day, they faced the questions: Is God trustworthy? Does he love us? Will he provide for us? Every time they answered "yes" to these questions, their faith grew a little stronger.

When Zechariah was struck mute by the angel (Luke 1:20), he entered an intense time of blessing from the Lord. God wanted to teach him, so that Zechariah could then teach his son what it meant to rely on God. When John was born, Zechariah's response bore witness to the fruit of his nine months of silence. Filled with the Holy Spirit, he proclaimed God's faithfulness and prophesied great blessings over his son.

How important this time was for Zechariah—and for the whole of salvation history! John was destined to spend years alone in the desert, listening to God and awaiting the time when he should appear and announce the Messiah's coming. Then, when he was imprisoned by Herod and awaiting his fate, John again needed to be sustained by all that God had promised. Where did he learn such patience and trust, if not from Zechariah and Elizabeth?

We all have unfulfilled desires and hopes. As beloved children of God, we must never give up hope. We can place our full confidence in the one who called us by name and hears the prayers that spring from our hearts. As we wait on the Lord, let us ask him to mold our characters and make us more like him. In the end, we will find that his plan is far better than our own. We will be able to proclaim with Zechariah that it was not by human power but by divine power that wonderful things have taken place in our lives.

Points for Meditation:

- Do you seek opportunities to be formed by God? Commit yourself to soaking up God's word in Scripture, either by spending time reading on your own or through a formal Bible study.

- Zechariah and Elizabeth carefully prepared their son John for his mission by living their faith and teaching him about the glory of the Lord. If you are a parent, what are some ways you can show your children how important it is to make God the center of their lives?
- In the birth of their son John, the plans and desires that Elizabeth and Zechariah had for their lives were fulfilled, but in a completely unexpected way and for an unanticipated purpose. In what practical ways can you imitate this couple in abandoning yourself to God's plans and God's timing—especially as it is unfolding right now in your life?

Prayer:

Father, you know everything about me. You never stop thinking about me and surrounding me with your love. You know what will truly fulfill me and give me peace. How wonderful are your ways!

JUNE 29

Sts. Peter and Paul, apostles

Solemnity

Vigil Mass:
Acts 3:1-10
Psalm 19:2-5
Galatians 1:11-20
John 21:15-19

Mass during the Day:
Acts 12:1-11
Psalm 34:2-9
2 Timothy 4:6-8,17-18
Matthew 16:13-19

I have fought the good fight, I have finished the race, I have kept the faith. (2 Timothy 4:7)

Since at least the year 354, this day has been set aside to honor the apostles Peter and Paul. The memory of these great apostles and our reverence for the work of grace in their lives have pierced the hearts of the faithful ever since. Of all the men and women who have ever lived, these two were chosen to be the apostles to the Jews and the Gentiles.

In Peter we see a hot-tempered, unschooled fisherman who became a bold, self-controlled preacher and pastor. Peter was so transformed by the Spirit that he was able to sleep soundly in the face of death! Luke tells us of an incident in which Herod had arrested Peter with the intention of beheading him (Acts 12:1-4). So complete was Peter's trust in God and his acceptance of God's plan that, in prison, on what could have been the last night of his life, he was able to sleep like a baby. The angel whom God sent to rescue Peter had to strike him on the side in order to wake him up (12:7)!

At a similar point in his life, Paul is depicted as being poured out as a libation for the Lord (Philippians 2:17). This former Pharisee, who had previously condemned and put to death Jesus' disciples, was so changed that he could accept his death and offer it to the Lord as an act of worship! He sought neither redress nor vindication, but was willing to offer his very life for the sake of the gospel. When his fate was certain, he remained calm, accepting, and ever-trusting in God's faithfulness.

God's power to transform his people is unlimited. Peter and Paul completely surrendered themselves to Jesus so that he could work through them to give birth to his church. When we surrender ourselves as Peter and Paul did, giving God permission to transform us and to use us as he sees fit, great things can happen. Even if the work we are called to do seems little in our own eyes, we should never underestimate its importance to God. Although Peter and Paul brought thousands of people to Christ, we build the kingdom even when we witness to just one person.

God is inviting every one of us to share in the calling of the apostles: to teach, to witness to the gospel, to love with the love of Jesus, to run the race. Let us pray for the church today, that God would give us the grace to be open to his transforming work.

Points for Meditation:

- Compare Peter before and after his transformation in the Holy Spirit by reading Matthew 26:69-75 and Acts 3. Think about the changes you have seen the Lord make in you as the Holy Spirit has become more active in your life. Give the Lord permission to transform you in an even greater way.

- How could Paul be so sure that he and all those who loved Jesus would receive a "crown of righteousness" (2 Timothy 4:8)? Why was he able to "let go" of the sins he had committed before his conversion? If you lack confidence that you will also win the same crown, search your heart for any unrepented sin, confess it to the Lord, and place it at the foot of the cross. Celebrate the Sacrament of Reconciliation. Then stand on Jesus' promise that through his blood, you will be saved.
- Much of the work of spreading the gospel is "hidden," done day in and day out but often unnoticed. If you are doing some "hidden" work for the Lord, like raising your children or teaching a catechism class, ask the Lord to give you a sense of how important this work is to him. Renew your commitment to building God's kingdom in whatever way he desires.

Prayer:

Lord Jesus, touch my heart with the power of your resurrection. Help all Christians pursue the unity which gives witness, in love, to the one faith we share in Christ.

JULY 3

St. Thomas, apostle

Feast

Ephesians 2:19-22
Psalm 117:1-2
John 20:24-29

"My Lord and my God!"
(John 20:28)

Thomas could not believe in Jesus' resurrection simply on the basis of what he heard: "Unless I see in his hands the print of the nails, and place my finger in the mark of the nails and place my hand in his side, I will not believe" (John 20:25). Perhaps we could fault Thomas for his stubborn refusal to believe. We feel we ought to be better than Thomas, not needing hard evidence to believe in Jesus. But we should not forget that God wants to show himself to us. He wants to have a personal relationship with each of us—something that goes deeper than our simply believing based on others' testimony.

Thomas is a marvelous sign of hope to us. In his doubts, Thomas was in a sense a "stranger and sojourner" (Ephesians 2:19). Yet, when he met the risen Lord, he became part of the "foundation of apostles and prophets" (2:20). In a homily on Thomas, St. Gregory the Great (c. 540-604) said:

> God's mercy arranged that the disbelieving disciple, in touching the wounds of his master's body, should heal our wounds of disbelief. . . . As he touches Christ and is won over to belief, every doubt is cast aside and our faith is strengthened. So the disciple who doubted, then felt Christ's wounds, becomes a witness to the reality of the resurrection. (*Homily 26*)

How good of the Lord to include in the company of his apostles one who disbelieved for a time. Thomas should encourage us that we too can ask to see Jesus and trust that he will show himself to us. In going from unbelief to belief, Thomas became the first to direct our attention to Jesus' wounds and their incredible power to change our faith and bring us healing.

Jesus' wounds represent his compassion, his love for us, and his desire to be near to us. The Holy Spirit wants to increase our faith. He wants to teach us that it is only through Jesus' wounds that we can be saved. Let us place our hope in Christ, who freed us from sin and death. Let us ask to see Jesus so that we can cry out with Thomas: "My Lord and my God!"

Points for Meditation:

- "With his stripes we are healed" (Isaiah 53:5). Meditate on this verse from Isaiah. How have you allowed the wounds of Christ to heal your sins and suffering?
- When he saw Jesus, Thomas not only believed that he had risen from the dead, he also proclaimed that Jesus was God—a knowledge that could only have come through faith. Do you permit your faith in Jesus to be weakened by those things you can physically see—like suffering or evils in the world? Ask the Lord to increase your faith in him, even when you don't understand why some things happen the way they do.
- We encounter Christ every time we receive him at Mass in the Eucharist. Do you hunger for Jesus? Ask the Lord to give you a greater appreciation and awe for the real presence of Christ in the Eucharist.

Prayer:

Jesus, let us know your presence this very day. Strengthen our faith and fill us with your love so that we can proclaim you to everyone we meet.

JULY 22

St. Mary Magdalene

Memorial

Song of Songs 3:1-4
or 1 Corinthians 5:14-17
Psalm 63:2-6,8-9
John 20:1-2,11-18

Jesus said to her, "Mary."
(John 20:16)

Mary Magdalene had been plagued by demons, and Jesus healed her. With gratitude, she joined the band of women who care for him (Luke 8:2-3) and was among those who followed him from Galilee to Jerusalem (Matthew 27:55-56), hearing his word every day and seeing his miracles. Finally, while many fled in fear, Mary Magdalene stood loyally near the cross—a true disciple to the end—and watched as Jesus shed his blood (John 19:25). But even that courageous act was not enough to satisfy her devotion.

Grief-stricken, Mary went to mourn at Jesus' grave, just to be close to his body. But sorrow was turned into joy when she encountered first an empty tomb and then Jesus, risen from the dead! Calling her by name, Jesus freed Mary again—this time from the despair that had overcome her as she watched him die. With a single word, "Mary," Jesus revived her. Mary's reply, "Rabboni!" or "Master!" contained not only relief and joy, but a pledge of faith in him and in his resurrection (John 20:16).

Jesus appeared not to the priests and rulers of Israel, not even to the men he had chosen as his closest companions, but to a woman with a disturbed past. What a great reward Mary Magdalene received! She was the first witness of the resurrection. Sharing her astonishing news with the other disciples, Mary became the "apostle to the apostles," a title preserved in the Byzantine tradition. She was the first herald of the resurrection.

Once again, God revealed himself to the lowly, to someone we would least expect. Whatever demonic bondage Mary had suffered—whether she had been mentally ill, trapped in sin, or afflicted with a debilitating illness like epilepsy—it did not matter to Jesus. Neither does he hold our past against us.

Jesus came for just this reason, to deliver us from the shame and sins of our past and to reconcile us with the Father. He calls us each by name to share in eternal life with him and transforms us through the power of his Holy Spirit so that we too can be witnesses to his resurrection.

Points for Meditation:

- During his earthly ministry, Jesus told his disciples to follow him. Mary Magdalene followed Jesus wherever he went—even to the cross and to the grave. Spend some time today in prayer thanking Jesus for calling you as well. Tell him you will follow him wherever he leads.
- Is there something in your past that continues to plague you and fill you with shame? Surrender it to Jesus at the foot of the cross. Hear Jesus say your name with the same compassion and love that he expressed when he said Mary's name.
- Jesus associated with tax collectors and sinners (Matthew 9:11), and chose a woman with a questionable past to be the first person on earth to witness his resurrection. Jesus obviously saw the dignity of each human being with whom he came into contact. Are we open to associating

with those who are considered outcasts? Can we share the good news with them? Do we see in each person, no matter what their station in life, their God-given dignity?

Prayer:

O Jesus, risen Lord and Savior, you are the hope of glory! My heart rejoices at the sound of your voice. Thank you for awakening new hope in me and lifting me up to new life in you.

JULY 25

St. James, apostle

Feast

2 Corinthians 4:7-15
Psalm 126:1-6
Matthew 20:20-28

Are you able to drink the cup that I am to drink? (Matthew 20:22)

Boanerges, or "sons of thunder," aptly described Jesus' impetuous disciples James and John, the sons of Zebedee (Mark 3:17). James and John, who were fishermen when Jesus called them, were prominent among the twelve disciples. They were both present with Jesus at important moments in his ministry: the raising of Jairus' daughter (Mark 5:37-43); Jesus' transfiguration (Matthew 17:1-2); and his time of darkness in the Garden of Gethsemane (Matthew 26:36-37).

The mother of these two disciples recognized her sons' importance to Jesus and asked him to grant them places of honor in the kingdom of heaven. It seems that she and her sons were seeking godly greatness according to worldly terms. Jesus responded: "You do not know what you are asking" (Matthew 20:22). When he questioned whether they would be able to drink the same "cup" that he was to drink, James and John confidently proclaimed that they could. However, they probably did not completely understand what this "cup" meant.

Jesus taught James that true discipleship was not achieved through power, authority, or recognition, but through humility, trust, obedience, and service. Although worthy of royal treatment when he entered the world, Jesus was born a helpless baby in a humble stable. Throughout his life, he trusted his Father for all his needs and never once drew attention to himself. He was recognized not because he was served, but because he performed the ultimate service: giving his life for our sins.

James learned his lesson well. A leader in the church at Jerusalem, he became a radiant light to Christ, witnessing not to his own power, but to the transcendent power of God (2 Corinthians 4:7). He also performed the ultimate service of martyrdom by order of King Herod Agrippa I (Acts 12:1-2).

We too obtain godly greatness through Jesus' death. On Calvary, Jesus put to death our fallen nature, and in his resurrection he opened the way for us to know his presence. We are earthen vessels filled with the glory of God. As we unite ourselves to Jesus' death, the glory of his resurrection will shine through us, making us witnesses to his love.

Points for Meditation:

- Jesus' answer to the mother of James and John spoke volumes about his Father's view of power and authority. In what ways are you able to be a servant-leader in the authority that you exercise in your life? How is God calling you to lay down your life for the good of others?
- St. Paul said, "While we live we are always being given up to death for Jesus' sake, so that the life of Jesus may be manifested in our mortal flesh" (2 Corinthians 4:11). From the moment James met Jesus to the time of his own martyrdom, this apostle was "being given up to death for Jesus' sake." Look at some of the struggles and challenges in your own life from the perspective that you are dying to self in order to be filled with the life of Jesus. How

does this change your outlook?

- Is there a "cup" you must drink in your life or in the life of someone you love? Ask the Lord for the strength to embrace his will in every situation, whatever the cost.

Prayer:

Lord, fill us with your presence. Teach us to lay our lives down for you so that we can bring your love and healing to others. Nothing in this world compares to the new life you have won for us.

JULY 29

St. Martha

Memorial

Gospel Reading:
John 11:19-27 or Luke 10:38-42

"Yes, Lord; I believe that you are the Christ, the Son of God, he who is coming into the world." (John 11:27)

How good it is to put our trust in God's faithfulness, even as we endure difficult periods of "waiting on the Lord." In Martha, Scripture shows us the witness of one who learned this lesson. We first see her confronting Jesus about her sister Mary's apparent laziness as Mary sat quietly at Jesus' feet (Luke 10:38-42). At that time, Jesus told her that Mary's posture of quiet listening was the "better portion." Then, some time later, after Jesus' firm but gentle rebuke began to sink in, we see Martha having to wait patiently as she watched her brother Lazarus die without any sign of Jesus' coming to heal or even comfort him.

With Lazarus dead and Jesus nowhere in sight, Martha didn't complain. It may have been difficult, but she put her faith in him. When Jesus finally did arrive, she didn't upbraid him. Instead, she confessed his ability "even now" to raise her brother. As a consequence, Martha's faith was richly rewarded.

While this story demonstrates the value of trusting in Jesus, it does not mean that we should always sit passively and "hope" everything will work out. There will be times in our lives when we feel God has forgotten us. Sometimes the sheer intensity or duration of a crisis can shake us to the core. Yet these are often the very opportunities God uses to build us up. Even if it doesn't seem so at the moment, God works everything for good for those who love him (Romans 8: 28). Our faith can grow as we fix our hearts on Jesus, do the best we can to follow him, and wait to see how he will act on our behalf.

Don't fear the future. Hold on to the fact that Jesus "has borne our griefs and carried our sorrows" (Isaiah 53:4). Even when you are called to participate in the sufferings of Jesus, you can do so knowing that through his blood, you have ultimate victory. Continue to exercise your faith, and your heart will open more and more to his provision. Jesus will never let you down.

Points for Meditation:

- Imagine you are Martha and your brother Lazarus has just died. Jesus says to you: "I am the resurrection and the life; he who believes in me, though he die, yet shall he live, and whoever lives and believes in me shall never die." Then he looks you straight in the eye and asks: "Do you believe this?" (John 11:25,26). What would you say to him?
- Right after Martha affirmed her faith in Jesus as the resurrection and the life, she warned him not to move away the stone because of the odor (John 11:39). Jesus again had to remind her, "Did I not tell you that if you would believe you would see the glory of God?" (11:40). How would you gauge the level of expectancy in your faith? Do you anticipate seeing God's glory as a result of your faith and prayers?
- If you are going through a difficult time of "waiting on the Lord," repeat to yourself the

promises of your faith. Your Father is a kind and loving God who cares about you beyond all comprehension. He sent his Son Jesus to suffer for you and redeem you. Jesus will never abandon you. He weeps with you in your sorrows and rejoices with you in your victories. You will live with him forever in his glory. Let these promises sink into the very core of your being so that they become the foundation of an unshakable faith.

Prayer:

Lord, as I wait for you, teach me prayers of intercession so that my faith can move mountains. Help me to persevere as I pray for my family, your church, and the world.

AUGUST 6

Transfiguration of the Lord

Feast

Daniel 7:9-10,13-14
Psalm 97:1-2,5-6,9
2 Peter 1:16-19
Cycle A: Matthew 17:1-9
Cycle B: Mark 9:2-10
Cycle C: Luke 9:28-36

*Peter said to Jesus, "Lord, it is well that we are here."
(Matthew 17:4)*

Jesus' transfiguration not only gave his disciples—and us—an awesome glimpse of his glory; it also gives us a glimpse of the transformation we will experience at the resurrection. On the last day, we too will be raised from the dead. Like Jesus on Mount Tabor, our bodies will be transfigured and glorified. We will live forever with the Lord in an embrace so close that his divine nature will transform every part of who we are. This, above everything else, is the basis for our hope in Christ. This is the heart of our faith as Christians.

Why is the transfiguration an important event? Because on that day, Peter, James, and John were given a "bird's eye view" of God's purposes and plans. There, accompanied by two of the greatest figures from Israel's history, Moses and Elijah, Jesus was revealed as the fulfillment of all God had done on the earth. Everything pointed to the glory of God that was destined to be shared with his people—with all who placed their faith in Jesus and listened to him (Matthew 17:5).

The three disciples who saw the glorified Lord were given a vision meant to strengthen them for the difficult days ahead when Jesus would be arrested and crucified. With this vision of Jesus as he would be after his resurrection, and with the Father's voice testifying to his Son, these disciples were able to see how God was thoroughly in control of all that would happen, both to Jesus and to themselves.

The promise of the transfiguration can be ours as well. We have the testimony of those who saw Jesus transformed (2 Peter 1:16), but even more importantly, each of us can experience a taste of the same vision that Peter, James, and John had. In our own prayer, we can fix our eyes on Jesus and know his touch. At Mass, as we kneel before the Blessed Sacrament, our hearts can be filled with the glory of the risen life that is ours in Christ. In your prayer today, ask Jesus to reveal himself more deeply to you. Let his hope banish all of your fears and anxieties.

Points for Meditation:

- The transfiguration was definitely a "mountaintop" spiritual experience for the disciples. However, instead of simply standing in awe and wonder, Peter anxiously suggested building three booths. Are you so used to *doing* that you have trouble just *being* in the presence of the Lord? In your prayer today, try to rid yourself of thoughts of what you should be doing for God and simply enjoy his presence and peace.
- Both before and after the transfiguration, Jesus told the disciples that he must go to Jerusalem and die at the hands of the elders (Matthew 16:21; 17:2; 17:22-23). The transfiguration helped the disciples to bear the sorrow of the cross because they saw the glory that lay ahead. Whenever you are bearing crosses, pray through

the Scripture passages on the transfiguration. Let Jesus' transfiguration fill you with a willingness to endure your present difficulties in order to gain the prize that awaits you.

- The words coming from the cloud at the transfiguration— "This is my beloved Son, with whom I am well pleased" Matthew 17:5)—are the same words spoken by the Father from heaven when Jesus was baptized in the Jordan (Mark 1:11). In both instances, the Father was expressing his pleasure in his Son, who was fulfilling his mission by beginning his earthly ministry and by facing his crucifixion. Ask yourself, "Am I confident in the mission God has for me?" If you are unsure of God's will for your life, spend extra time in prayer asking that he reveal it to you.

Prayer:

Jesus, how good it is to be here with you. Let me never lose sight of your glory, no matter how much darkness may press on me. Let me live in your presence forever.

AUGUST 10

St. Lawrence, deacon and martyr

Feast

2 Corinthians 9:6-10
Psalm 112:1-2,5-9
John 12:24-26

Truly, truly, I say to you, unless a grain of wheat falls into the earth and dies, it remains alone; but if it dies, it bears much fruit. (John 12:24)

Lawrence was a third-century Roman deacon who served the Lord and laid down his life for God's glory. As one of the seven deacons serving the Christians in Rome, Lawrence was responsible for distributing alms to the poor. In 257, the Emperor Valerian published edicts against Christians, and the following year, Pope Sixtus II was put to death. Four days later, Lawrence met the same end.

According to tradition, when told by the Roman authorities to hand over the treasures of the church, Lawrence gathered the poor, the disabled, and the sick and brought them before the official. "These are the treasures of the church," he said. And his fate was sealed. On August 10, 258, Lawrence was bound to a gridiron and slowly burned to death. His martyrdom inspired great devotion in the city of Rome. When the persecutions ended, a church was built over his tomb and many miracles were attributed to his intercession.

Like many saints, Lawrence personified the words of Jesus: "He who loves his life loses it, and he who hates his life in this world will keep it for eternal life" (John 12:25). Lawrence was a grain of wheat that died but bore much fruit for the Lord. His love for God was so great that he was willing to serve him in any way he could, even to death. Lawrence not only became like the poor he served, but like Jesus, he became the poorest of all.

When we love someone passionately, we are willing to do anything for that person. Every day we have the opportunity to love Jesus in such a way—with our whole heart, mind, and strength. Every day, as we wake up, we can ask him: "Lord, what would you have me do today? How can I love you today?" He may ask us to minister to the poor and needy, just as Lawrence did. As Lawrence knew so well, and as Mother Teresa said so often, the outcasts of society are Christ in the distressing disguise of poverty. No wonder Lawrence called them the treasures of the church!

Points for Meditation:

- St. Lawrence called the poor and sick of Rome the "treasures" of the church. How does viewing the poor and needy in this way change the way you think of them? How does viewing yourself as a "treasure" of the church change the way you think of yourself in relation to God?
- God asks us for our time, talent, and treasure to build his kingdom. In what ways are you using your time, talent, and treasure to help the poor or to build up your church community? Are you the "cheerful giver" described by St. Paul? (2 Corinthians 9:7).
- St. Lawrence was so peaceful about his impending martyrdom that he was said to have joked with his persecutors. As you recall God's promises of eternal life with him and his Spirit's

presence in you now, try to imagine yourself in Lawrence's predicament. Imagine yourself overcoming your fears of death through faith in Christ.

Prayer:

Father, thank you for your saints. They have shown us the way to you. Keep the witness of their love in our hearts and minds, so that we may be ready to love and serve others as they did.

AUGUST 15

Assumption of the Blessed Virgin Mary

Solemnity

Vigil:
1 Chronicles 15:3-4,15-16; 16:1-2
Psalm 132:6-7,9-10,13-14
1 Corinthians 15:54-57
Luke 11:27-28

Mass during the Day:
Revelation 11:19; 12:1-6,10
Psalm 45:10-12,16
1 Corinthians 15:20-26
Luke 1:39-56

My soul magnifies the Lord, and my spirit rejoices in God my Savior. (Luke 1:46-47)

Mary's whole being glorified and rejoiced in God her Savior. Throughout her entire life, as a true daughter of Zion, she did most perfectly what God's own chosen people failed to do: She desired God's will and sought to live it (Luke 1:38). God rewarded her by assuming her, body and soul, into heaven.

We should see Mary in light of the whole work of God. He created the human race in order to have a people with whom he could share his love. But the people chose to live for themselves; they refused to live as his people. A flood destroyed all but the righteous, and from the descendants of these righteous few, God chose for himself a people through Abraham.

God worked with this chosen people he called Israel, sending them priests, prophets, and kings to guide them. Still, sin corrupted them and they went their own way. What could not be accomplished through his people because of their willfulness, God did in his Son Jesus through his loving obedience.

Mary was a member of the people chosen by God. But as a faithful daughter of Zion, she glorified and rejoiced in God in a singular way. She did what God wanted all his people to do (Luke 11:27-28). God knew her heart in advance and so worked in her in an extraordinary way, preserving her from sin so that she would be a worthy vessel to carry and care for his divine Son. Through this Son, all people would be drawn together into the Israel of God and be presented to the Father as the people who would love and serve him.

The assumption of Mary is a sign to the world of what awaits all who respond to God. Mary was taken into heaven to live in the presence of the Lord. What has happened in her life will happen in the lives of all who—like her—live singularly for God (1 Corinthians 15:20-25). Her life is a sign that this work is possible when we allow God to work in us according to his plan.

Let us pray that in our beings we would glorify and rejoice in God our Savior. May we be true children of Zion, desiring God's will and seeking to live it.

Points for Meditation:

- Think about your day-to-day existence. What is its main purpose? What does it mean for you to live single-mindedly for God?
- While it may be difficult to imagine what it is like to have a resurrected body, there are passages from Scripture describing the risen Christ that can help us to grasp more fully what we will someday experience for ourselves. Read first of

Jesus' transfiguration, which was a foreshadowing of his resurrection (Matthew 17:1-8; Mark 9:2-8). Then meditate on the following passages: Mark 16; Luke 24; and John 20-21.

- Consider the trust in God that was required of Mary through the major events in her life: being found with child before her marriage; delivering her baby in a cave far from home; having to flee to Egypt with her husband and newborn; watching her son die an unjust death. What events in your own life have required that kind of trust? How were you able to see God's purposes fulfilled through these events?

Prayer:

Lord Jesus, we pray for all those who do not yet hope for the resurrection. May each person come to know that the reason we have been created is to live with you for all eternity.

AUGUST 24

St. Bartholomew, apostle

Feast

Revelation 21:9-14
Psalm 145:10-13,17-18
John 1:45-51

Truly, truly, I say to you, you will see heaven opened, and the angels of God ascending and descending upon the Son of man. (John 1:51)

John is the only gospel writer to mention the apostle Nathanael, but tradition considers him to be the "Bartholomew" of the other gospels. His name means "son of Tolmai" and could have been Nathanael's surname. Another clue to his identity lies in the fact that Bartholomew is always listed beside the name of Philip, the one who John tells us introduced Nathanael to Jesus (John 1:45-46). Popular traditions and legends say that Nathanael preached in some of the most hostile countries of the East—India, Ethiopia, and Persia—and eventually died in Armenia, where he was flayed alive, then beheaded or possibly crucified.

When Philip shared his belief that Jesus of Nazareth might well be the Messiah, Nathanael replied, "Can anything good come out of Nazareth?" (John 1:46). Rabbinical thinking held that the Messiah would come from Judea, the land of David—most certainly not from a region such as Galilee, which was overrun by the Gentiles. More than a cynical remark or statement of unbelief, Nathanael's reaction revealed a firm adherence to God's word as he understood it and a willingness to have his assumptions challenged and his faith stretched. The fact that he accepted Philip's invitation to meet Jesus says much about Nathanael's openness to seeking the truth.

With fitting irony, having never spoken a word with Nathanael, Jesus declared, "Behold, an Israelite indeed, in whom is no guile!" (John 1:47). Nathanael's openness to the truth impressed Jesus. This man didn't hide behind masks when dealing with other people. Instead, he spoke truthfully (sometimes bluntly) and expected nothing less in return. Nathanael's honest, open heart must have been fertile ground indeed for God's word to take root. His confession that Jesus was the Son of God was only the beginning. As Jesus himself promised, he would see heaven opened!

God wants to give us the same freedom and openness that Nathanael had. Being without guile is not just a natural attribute, but can come to us as we place our security more and more in the hands of Jesus. Knowing his forgiveness and trusting in his Father's provision, we will have no need for the defenses and cynical self-protection that seem so much a part of this world. Like Nathanael, let us immerse ourselves in Scripture and let the word of God heal us of all guile.

Points for Meditation:

- Jesus said that he saw Nathanael under the fig tree, even before Philip brought him along to meet Jesus. What do you think it was about this simple statement that prompted Nathanael to proclaim the truth about Jesus as the Messiah? Do you believe that Jesus knows you to the very core of your being, and that he knew you even before you gave your life to him? How does this belief strengthen your faith?

- Someone who is free of guile might be considered rather naive. Do you think that some measure of guile, which is defined as cunning or deceit, is necessary to survive in the world? Ask the Lord to free you from any fears you might have of being vulnerable or unprotected. Ask him to replace these fears with a strong sense of his protection.
- Do you hold on to any preconceived notions about God which might limit your openness to his working in your life? For example, do you think your concerns are too insignificant to be brought before the Lord? Do you believe that you are unworthy for God to hear you and speak to you? Whatever false assumptions you might harbor, renounce them now and ask Jesus to reveal his truths to you.

Prayer:

Lord, you know us better than we know ourselves. May your Spirit remove our guile and make us lights that clearly reflect your glory.

AUGUST 29

Beheading of St. John the Baptist

Memorial

Jeremiah 1:17-19
Psalm 71:1-6,15,17
Mark 6:17-29

Herod feared John, knowing that he was a righteous and holy man. (Mark 6:20)

The embodiment of radicalism, John the Baptist dressed in camel's hair, "ate locusts and wild honey" (Mark 1:6), and prepared the way for Jesus by boldly exhorting people to repent and be baptized for the forgiveness of sins (Mark 1:4). All during his life, John stood as a prefigurement of Jesus, the one he heralded. An angel foretold both of their births and named both of them (Luke 1:13,31; Isaiah 49:1). They were both conceived as a result of God's miraculous intervention (Luke 1:24-25,35). Even in infancy, people recognized God's hand upon them (Luke 1:66; 2:18-19).

Both John and Jesus "grew and became strong in spirit," and each spent time alone before beginning his public ministry (Luke 1:80; 2:40; Mark 1:12-13). The Lord made both their mouths like sharp swords (Isaiah 49:2), able to cut through the deceptions of human reasoning with the truths of repentance, forgiveness, and God's loving call to bear "fruits worthy of repentance" (Luke 3:8; Matthew 7:21). John willingly suffered and died for Jesus, just as Jesus died so that all people could become children of God.

Of John the Baptist, St. Bede the Venerable said: "Such was the quality and strength of the man who accepted the end of this present life by shedding his blood." Through he was "locked away in the darkness of prison . . . [he] deserved to be called a bright and shining lamp" by Christ, "the Light of life" (*Homilies*, 23).

As the Holy Spirit's temple, we too are called to be bright lights, glorifying Christ in a world darkened by sin. Although we probably will not experience martyrdom, we can daily imitate Christ by following the Spirit's guidance instead of the inclinations of the flesh. Our radicalness may result in suffering, but our hearts will overflow with joy as the Spirit enables us, like Jesus, to triumph over death. Despite difficulties, we will rejoice as we see Jesus reborn into the world through our witness.

Points for Meditation:

- The gospel message is attractive, because of the hope it gives, but also disturbing, because of the way it challenges us. Herod was attracted to John's message, but was unable to turn away from the sin in his life. What character traits or weaknesses hindered Herod in following through with his initial attraction to John's preaching? Is there something similar in your life that prevents you from following the Lord more closely?
- John was never fearful about proclaiming the truth, regardless of the consequences. When you have the opportunity to stand up for the truth, do you experience fear of persecution or suffering? In your prayer today, ask Jesus to deliver you from any fears you might have about proclaiming God's message of salvation.
- John the Baptist's knowledge of God produced a powerful humility in him. When asked if he were the Christ, John replied that he was not

even worthy to untie the Lord's sandals (John 1:27). Why was John's humility so essential to the mission God had given to him to herald the coming of Jesus? How can growth in humility help us to better fulfill God's will in our own lives?

Prayer:

God our Father, you called John the Baptist to be the herald of your Son's birth and death. As he gave his life in witness to truth and justice, so may we strive to profess our faith in your gospel. (*Opening Prayer for the Memorial*)

SEPTEMBER 8

Birth of Mary

Feast

Micah 5:1-4 or Romans 8:28-30
Psalm 13:6
Matthew 1:1-16,18-23

I will sing to the LORD, because he has dealt bountifully with me. (Psalm 13:6)

How wonderful that God, who is all powerful, would not condemn us in our sin, but would provide a way of salvation! How wonderful, even more, that he would call a "lowly handmaid"—the Blessed Virgin Mary—to participate in this plan. Today is a great feast because we recall how God's plan to share his glory with us took a decisive step toward completion.

Since the sixth century, the birthplace of Mary—which according to tradition is in Jerusalem—has been venerated. In the twelfth century, a church was built over this site, known as the Church of St. Anne, in honor of Mary's mother. The date of September 8 was chosen to celebrate Mary's birth because it is exactly nine months after December 8, the feast of the Immaculate Conception. Contemplating the wonder of the gospel and Mary's role in its completion, St. Andrew of Crete (c. 660-740) offered the following words:

> This is the highest, all-embracing benefit that Christ has bestowed on us. This is the revelation of the mystery, this is the emptying out of the divine nature, the union of God and man, and the deification of the manhood that was assumed. This radiant and manifest coming of God to men most certainly needed a joyful prelude to introduce the great gift of salvation to us. The present festival, the birth of the Mother of God, is a prelude, while the final act is the foreordained union of the Word with flesh. Today the Virgin is born, tended and formed, and prepared for her role as Mother of God, who is the universal King of the ages.
>
> Justly then do we celebrate this mystery since it signifies for us a double grace. We are led toward the truth, and we are led away from

our condition of slavery to the letter of the law. How can this be? Darkness yields before the coming of light, and grace exchanges legalism for freedom. But midway between the two stands today's mystery, at the frontier where types and symbols give way to reality, and the old is replaced by the new.

Therefore, let all creation sing and dance and unite to make worthy contribution to the celebration of this day. Let there be one common festival for saints in heaven and men on earth. Let everything in heaven and earth join in festive celebration. Today this created world is raised to the dignity of a holy place for him who made all things. The creature is newly prepared to be a divine dwelling place for the Creator.

Points for Meditation:

- Mary's "yes" to God has made it possible for us, each day, to repeat that "yes" to God's will in our lives. Spend time today thinking about the role that God has called you to play in the building of his kingdom. Don't let the devil convince you that you are too insignificant to be a part of God's plan.

- Mary's place at the end of the genealogy in the first chapter of the Gospel of Matthew is a powerful witness to God's faithfulness. God prepared his people for the promised Messiah, and Mary never doubted that God would fulfill his promises to her and to his people. When setbacks and challenges discourage you, is it because your hope is misplaced? How often do you become impatient with waiting on the Lord for his own timing?
- Mary's maternal care for her pilgrim children on earth has been manifested many times in the appearances she has made on earth, such as in Fatima and Lourdes. Her messages always speak of repentance and conversion to her Son. In your prayer today, tell Jesus that you want to renounce sin. Ask for the grace of a change of heart that will help you to follow him more closely.

Prayer:

Father, we praise you for your plan to make us like yourself! May we pray with your servant Mary, who said, "Let it be to me according to your word" (Luke 1:38).

SEPTEMBER 14

Triumph of the Cross

Feast

Numbers 21:4-9
Psalm 78:1-2,34-38
Philippians 2:6-11
John 3:13-17

And being found in human form he humbled himself and became obedient unto death, even death on a cross. Therefore God has highly exalted him and bestowed on him the name which is above every name. (Philippians 2:8-9)

Try to imagine the paradox: The cross, an instrument of extreme cruelty and disgrace, has become God's instrument of triumph and glory. With the battle over sin and death accomplished, Jesus now sits exalted in glory at the right hand of the Father. Because of Jesus' submission to the will of the Father, even to the point of death, he has won the victory of all victories. His death put an end to death. His suffering has dispelled our darkness. By Jesus' victory, God's plan is accomplished. Jesus' last words from the cross—"It is finished" (John 19:30)—rang out as a proclamation that the old creation, grown weak and tired in sin, was ended. A new creation in his risen life was about to begin, and we are all heirs of that new creation—the people he won through his death on the cross.

We who have been "bitten" by the serpent and have the poison of sin in our veins are called to look with faith upon the crucified one and be healed (Numbers 21:4-9). We are invited to look at Jesus' wounds, to gaze at the blood flowing from his side, from his hands, his feet, and his head. Through these wounds, healing of infinite magnitude is granted to the human race.

If we want to know the healing power of the cross, we must first come to the end of our own resources and striving for perfection. The cross tells us we cannot rid ourselves of sin; we cannot make ourselves acceptable to God. It is only in dying to ourselves, in handing our lives to God in total trust and submission, that we will experience the healing of the cross. The promise is that if we die with him, we will live with him (2 Timothy 2:11-12).

Today we honor the cross. We honor the Father for sending his Son to us. We honor Jesus, whose blood has won eternal victory for us. We honor the Spirit, who enables us to receive the grace poured out for us on the cross. This feast day is indeed among the brightest days of all human history.

Points for Meditation:

- Think of a victory celebration in which you may have participated. Perhaps your favorite football team won the Super Bowl or your local candidate won an election. Think of the happiness you felt at that moment. How much more does God want us to cheer and praise our King for enduring the cross and freeing us from sin and death! In prayer today, be sure to praise God for what he has done for you in Christ.
- Every day we face pressures and temptations that can raise doubts in our minds as to whether we really do share in Jesus' triumph over sin. Gaze upon a crucifix and affirm in your mind and heart the victory and power of the cross in your life. Pray the following Scripture verse: "For

the word of the cross is folly to those who are perishing, but to us who are being saved it is the power of God" (1 Corinthians 1:18).

- St. Paul tells us that Jesus "emptied himself" to become man and "humbled himself" to die on the cross (Philippians 2:6-7). If we are to share in the life of Christ, we must do the same so that we can also share in Christ's glory. Pray about what you need to "empty" in yourself—whether it be worldly desires, anger and resentment, or a hardened heart. Tell Jesus you want to share in his death so that you can know his resurrection.

Prayer:

Holy Spirit, open my eyes to see how you bring forth life from death and hope from suffering. Help me acknowledge my need for the healing power of the cross. Help me to trust in God's ability to bring me to victory over sin and death.

SEPTEMBER 15

Our Lady of Sorrows

Memorial

Hebrews 5:7-9
Psalm 31:2-6,15-16,20
John 19:25-27 or Luke 2:33-35

Behold, this child is set for the fall and rising of many in Israel, and for a sign that is spoken against (and a sword will pierce through your own soul also), that thoughts out of many hearts may be revealed. (Luke 2:34-35)

Consider the many sorrows Mary endured. She probably suffered ridicule and suspicion over her untimely pregnancy. She gave birth to her child, not in the familiar surroundings of home, but in a cave in a foreign city. Then, shortly after giving birth, she was forced to flee Israel altogether because of Herod's rage.

Mary was a real mother facing the challenges of life in the real world. She cooked, cleaned, changed diapers, taught her son, cared for her husband, loved her neighbors, gave to beggars, and went to bed tired, only to get up early and repeat the routine all over again. Yet it was in this environment, in the obscurity of her home, that she grew in holiness. Widowed early, Mary was already by herself when her son began his ministry. How difficult it must have been to let him go! She would have to watch from a distance as he poured out his life for perfect strangers, some of whom would turn on him. Any mother who has watched her children leave and worried about their future can understand Mary's concern.

Mary's heart was pierced a final time on Calvary, when she watched her son die a horrible death. What grief could be greater than receiving the dead body of her son in her arms? Who could ever share more fully than Mary in Jesus' sacrificial offering for a sin-sick world? Michelangelo's sculpture, the *Pietà*, shows Mary holding Jesus' body after his death. In the sculpture, she does not clutch him to her breast but holds him in her lap in a way that invites us to join her, both in her grief and in her consolation that he will rise for us all.

To all of us who have lost a child or suffer separation from loved ones, Mary continues to give us her Son. She continues to teach us to release our children into God's hands, because she knows that he who raised Christ Jesus from the dead can most certainly give life to us and our children.

Points for Meditation:

- As she held her dead son's body and wept, little did Mary know what joy she would feel just three days later when her son had risen from the dead. "Thou hast turned for me my mourning into dancing; thou hast loosed my sackcloth and girded me with gladness" (Psalm 30:11). If you have lost loved ones, ask the Lord to fill you with hope that you will one day rejoice with them in heaven.
- Mary never abandoned Jesus but remained "standing by the cross" (John 19:25) as he suffered and died. If you are sometimes tempted to abandon Jesus when difficulties confront you because you think that he has abandoned you, remember Mary at the foot of the cross. Unite yourself to Jesus and stand on his promises.

Mary is called Our Lady of Sorrows because of the way she joined her heart to the heart of God. As she saw her son suffering, she grasped how deeply the Father's heart was aching out of love for his wayward people. Like Mary, join your heart to the Father's and pray in intercession for all those who remain lost and far from God. Pray especially for those in your family who did not know the Lord.

Prayer:

Mary, you are the mother to all who turn to you. I come to you as my mother and ask you to protect my children and all the children of the world.

SEPTEMBER 21

St. Matthew, apostle and evangelist

Feast

Ephesians 4:1-7,11-13
Psalm 19:2-5
Matthew 9:9-13

Those who are well have no need of a physician, but those who are sick. (Matthew 9:12)

Imagine Matthew sitting at his customs post along the road that passed Capernaum, totally absorbed in his work. In the opinion of the Jewish farmers and fishermen who had to pay him a toll to carry their products down the road to market, Matthew probably seemed like a traitor. He was raising taxes for the regime that held them in subjection. In addition, tax collectors were known to enrich themselves by charging higher fees than they were required to turn over to the government. Thus, Matthew was probably regarded as a thief as well. Tax collectors were barred from the synagogue, just like robbers and murderers.

Jesus had just healed a man of paralysis and, as he left Capernaum, he had to walk by Matthew's toll office. Probably to Matthew's astonishment—certainly to the astonishment of Jesus' followers—Jesus went up to Matthew and invited him to become a disciple! We can only imagine what went through Matthew's mind. No doubt he had heard about Jesus before this encounter. Perhaps, like Zacchaeus, his fellow tax collector (Luke 19:1-4), Matthew had stood on the periphery of the crowd and listened to Jesus. Had his heart been touched by what he heard? Had Matthew asked himself, "Who is this man, Jesus?" Did he feel some vague desire to break free of the sin of his outcast way of life?

We cannot read Matthew's thoughts, but we know that this worldly man did not delay a minute in responding to Jesus' invitation. As soon as Jesus said, "Follow me," Matthew got up and followed (Matthew 9:9). By day's end, Matthew invited Jesus to join him and his fellow tax collectors at a dinner in his home (Luke 5:29).

Jesus saw Matthew as he sees all of us—not just for who we are, but for who we can become through his grace. Jesus loved Matthew and had a specific task waiting for him in the kingdom. Jesus turned this hated, hardened tax collector into an apostle of love. No personal transformation is impossible with God!

According to tradition, Matthew preached the gospel among the Jews for fifteen years after Jesus' resurrection, and then went on to evangelize in Persia, Macedonia, and Syria. After walking with Jesus on earth and witnessing his resurrection, this apostle faithfully poured out his life preaching the gospel of mercy that bears his name. May each of us who have experienced God's mercy be compelled by this same mercy to give it to others.

Points for Meditation:

- When Jesus called Matthew, he didn't choose someone who was already perfect. Do you think that you have to be perfect before you can come into the presence of Jesus or give your life to him? Ask Jesus to remove any feelings of unworthiness that may be keeping you separated from him. Trust that as you grow in your relationship with Jesus, you too will experience the kind of transformation that Matthew did.

- The tax collectors and other "public" sinners in Jesus' day could see that they were in need of a physician. The Pharisees, however, could not acknowledge their condition and so would not come to the Great Physician for healing. Do you see yourself as a sinner in need of redemption? Let go of any tendency to think you're doing "well enough" or to make light of sin. Tell Jesus how much you need him to cleanse you each day of your sinfulness.
- In his wildest dreams, Matthew probably never could have imagined quitting his job as a tax collector and becoming a missionary and evangelist. Yet while Matthew's skills were in tax collecting, he nonetheless accepted God's plan for his life. Ask the Lord to show you whether he is calling you to some distinct mission in your life. Even if it seems beyond your capabilities, ask him for the grace to carry it out.

Prayer:

Jesus, thank you for calling me to leave behind my selfish ways and follow you. Give me the grace to respond to you today without hesitation. Change me as much as you changed Matthew!

SEPTEMBER 29

Sts. Michael, Gabriel and Raphael, archangels

Feast

Daniel 7:9-10,13-14 or Revelation 12:7-12
Psalm 138:1-5
John 1:47-51

Truly, truly, I say to you, you will see heaven opened, and the angels of God ascending and descending upon the Son of man. (John 1:51)

Do you believe in angels? The church has always affirmed their existence. The *Catechism of the Catholic Church* tells us that angels are created spiritual beings with intellects and wills and that each angel is a unique and immortal heavenly being (CCC, 327-336).

The functions of the three archangels correspond to three major thrusts of Jesus' ministry:

bringing the good news, healing the sick, and delivering the oppressed. Gabriel, whose name means "God is mighty," is God's main messenger, bringing good news to his people. He announced to Mary that she would give birth to the Savior. Raphael, whose name means "God heals," is associated with healing (Tobit 12:1-22). Michael, whose name means "one who is like God," delivers God's people from oppression by doing battle with Satan (Revelation 12:7)

Though humans are "for a little while lower than angels," our destiny is to be divinized in Christ and raised above the angels (Psalm 8:4-6). Scripture tells us that Lucifer and a third of the angels in heaven rebelled against God (Revelation 12:3-9) out of envy (Wisdom 2:23-24) because we were to be the "first fruits" of all God created (James 1:18). So, if we want to protect ourselves, we need to remember that the spiritual battle we face is real. While Jesus has already defeated Satan and his fallen angels, they are still free to tempt and test us until Jesus comes in glory.

In the midst of this daily spiritual battle, let us be aware of the fight between good and evil. By understanding the seriousness of this battle and how it can affect us, we can arm ourselves with the assurance that, through Jesus, we are incorporated into the Trinity. In Christ, nothing can overcome us; we can claim victory against every attack. God's angels are always available to minister to our needs (Hebrews 1:14). As we celebrate the feast of the archangels today, let us wrap ourselves in Jesus' love, ask his angels to help us, and thank God for his awesome provision for us.

Points for Meditation:

- On three occasions in the Gospel of Matthew, Jesus spoke about angels and their care (Matthew 4:11; 18:10; and 26:53). Read these passages. How do you see angels fitting into God's plan for the world and his creation?
- Angels are part of the spiritual realm around us, and they confront the invisible powers of evil in the world. If you suspect Satan or his forces are at work trying to undermine something positive in your life or in the life of someone you love, ask for angelic help and pray for "deliverance from evil."
- Jesus is the point of contact between heaven and earth. Do you believe that through faith in Christ and baptism in his name, the heavens can

be opened to you every day? Think of past times when you have experienced the "heavenly life"—a strong sense of God's presence or his healing, forgiveness, or love. Thank the Lord for his faithfulness.

Prayer:

Father, I praise you for the glory and splendor of your angels. Let them assist me in my journey back to you. Jesus, open the heavens for me. Let me see the realities of the spiritual realm all around me. Help me fix my eyes on you and my heavenly inheritance.

OCTOBER 2

Guardian Angels

Memorial

Exodus 23:20-23
Psalm 91:1-6,10-11
Matthew 18:1-5,10

For he will give his angels charge of you to guard you in all your ways. (Psalm 91:11)

Guardian angels are those spiritual beings privileged to gaze upon God and worship him even as they watch over us and safeguard us. St. Basil the Great, one of the earliest doctors of the church, wrote, "Beside each believer stands an angel as protector and shepherd leading him to life." In addition, the church teaches that "By God's providence, angels have been entrusted with the office of guarding the human race and of accompanying every human being so as to preserve him from any serious dangers. Our heavenly Father has placed over each of us an angel under whose protection and vigilance we are" (*St. Pius IV Catechism*, IV,9,4).

While we often consider talk of guardian angels the stuff of myth and wishful thinking, the truth of their existence is yet one more piece of evidence of God's love for us. He has given each one of us an angel—a pure spirit—to watch out for us. We can find great comfort and security in knowing that not a hair falls from our head without our Father's knowledge (Matthew 10:30).

It can be so easy to get caught up in the concerns and anxieties of the day and lose sight of the great love that surrounds us. We are often quick to forget our heritage as sons and daughters of a God who has covenanted himself to us. Still, God remains faithful and is always weighing and measuring his provision according to our needs.

Recalling God's blessings can build up our confidence in him and keep us from wavering in our trust in him when things don't go our way. Remembering how God has cared for us helps us live "like children" (Matthew 18:3)—trusting in his provision, seeking his will, and thanking him for his mercy. Why not pray your own litany of praise and thanksgiving today? Remind yourself of the many good things God has done for you. Let your memory and imagination work together to lift you up to God's throne.

Points for Meditation:

- As children, we readily believe in the existence of a guardian angel, but as we grow older, we often become more cynical about the closeness of God and the reality of his angelic guardians. We may even begin to believe that we are the masters of our fate and have no one to help us but ourselves. Ask Jesus to free you from any sense of isolation or self-sufficiency that may be holding you back. Ask for a deeper dependence on the Lord.
- Think of specific occurrences in your life when you felt that your guardian angel was watching over you and protecting you, either from physical danger or from serious sin. Thank your Father in heaven for his protection and love.
- Think about any fears you may have, whether for yourself or for a loved one. Then meditate slowly on Psalm 91. Claim God's promise of protection.

Prayer:

Father, you have blessed me so much, I will never be able to recount all your graces! I thank you for taking care of me and for sending your angel to watch over me. May I come to share your life with all the angels, singing your praises forever!

OCTOBER 18

St. Luke, evangelist

Feast

2 Timothy 4:9-17
Psalm 145:10-13,17-18
Luke 10:1-9

The harvest is plentiful, but the laborers are few; pray therefore the Lord of the harvest to send out laborers into his harvest. (Luke 10:2)

Jesus sent out his disciples to prepare for the harvest. Luke—a well-educated gentile Christian, physician, and companion of Paul—was such a worker. Author of the third gospel and of the Acts of the Apostles, Luke wrote primarily for gentile Christians to show them that they, as well as the Jews, were included in God's plan. What inspired Luke to give up his career and become a worker in the harvest—and follow a zealous Jew right into jail?

Though probably not an eyewitness to the events of Jesus' life (Luke 1:1-2), Luke had certainly met Christ through the preaching of the gospel and had experienced the power of the Holy Spirit in his life. In Jesus, Luke had found something worth living for, something worth sharing with others at the cost of his career and comfort. In Acts 1:8, Luke recounts Jesus' promise that the apostles would become his witnesses throughout the world. Although he was not one of the first apostles, Luke nevertheless displayed great faithfulness to this command through his devoted service to Paul.

In the gospel that bears his name, Luke consistently presented Jesus as he had come to know him. He stressed the Lord's gentleness and kindness, especially toward sinners and outcasts. Memorable stories of divine mercy, such as the prodigal son and Zacchaeus, are found in his gospel (Luke 15:11-32; 19:1-10). Always stressing mercy, Luke also wrote of the universal salvation Jesus came to bring. He wanted all of his readers to know that they had been included in God's plan of salvation. He devoted his life to demonstrating that Jesus is always available to those who turn to him.

Luke also assigned a prominent place to prayer.

In the Book of Acts, he depicted the disciples not only praying for guidance in important decisions (Acts 1:24), but also as part of their day-to-day life together (2:42). Throughout this book, Luke showed how the Holy Spirit guided the emerging church through prayer (4:31; 8:15; 13:1-3; 20:23). A prayerful man himself and a faithful servant, Luke stands before us today as a witness of what can happen to those who surrender their lives to Jesus.

Points for Meditation

- Luke was a writer and historian who gave much attention to dates and to accurate detail. Read chapters 27 and 28 of Acts of the Apostles as an adventure story. Notice that Luke writes these chapters in the first person. Imagine in your mind the scene of the shipwreck and take note of how Luke and Paul had to rely on the Lord throughout their ordeal.
- In his second Letter to Timothy, Paul refers to Luke as his only companion (2 Timothy 4:11). Luke and Paul were brothers in Christ who remained steadfast in their friendship and service for the sake of Jesus. Christianity is not only about our individual salvation but also about

growing in genuine love for the people of God. Are there opportunities in your life to stand by others as faithfully as Luke stood by Paul? Have you been able to make room in your life to love others sacrificially?

- As a laborer in the harvest, Luke bore fruit through his evangelistic and missionary work. We are called to proclaim the truth of Jesus in the many situations in which we find ourselves. Ask the Holy Spirit to guide you, as he did the first disciples, to those places where he wants you to be his laborer. Pray for an open heart, to be able to do whatever it is the Lord is calling you to do.

Prayer:

Father, thank you for the witness of Luke's devotion to your guidance. As you guided the early church through prayer, we ask that you guide us by your Holy Spirit. Lord, teach us to pray.

OCTOBER 28

Sts. Simon and Jude, apostles

Feast

Ephesians 2:19-22
Psalm 19:2-5
Luke 6:12-16

You are fellow citizens with the saints and members of the household of God, built upon the foundation of the apostles and prophets, Christ Jesus himself being the cornerstone.
(Ephesians 2:19-20)

Apart from a listing of their names as among the apostles chosen by Jesus (Luke 6:15-16), Scripture tells us precious little about Saints Simon and Jude. We do know that Simon was referred to as the "zealot," which meant that he was a member of a political party in Palestine that sought the end of Roman occupation of Israel. Jude was known as the son of James (Acts 1:13). Tradition holds that they traveled to Persia, where they converted many people and were eventually martyred.

Even though we don't know much about Simon and Jude, the church honors them as saints because they responded in faith to Jesus' invitation and were among the first eyewitnesses to God's plan of salvation. The *Catechism of the Catholic Church* teaches that the church "is apostolic because she is founded on the apostles" (CCC, 857). The church was built on the foundation of the teaching of apostles like Simon and Jude—people whose lives were radically transformed by the experience of the risen Christ.

During Jesus' last supper with his disciples, Jude asked him, "Lord, how is it that you will manifest yourself to us, and not to the world?" (John 14:22). Jesus responded with a promise. Those who love him and keep his word would receive an indescribable blessing: The Father and the Son would come to live within them (14:23). The fulfillment of this promise in Simon, Jude, and the other apostles made it possible for them to spread the gospel and "make disciples of all nations" (Matthew 28:19).

All members of the church share in this apostolic mission (CCC, 863). Equally, for all members, "the fruitfulness of apostolate for ordained ministers as well as for lay people clearly depends on their vital union with Christ" (864). Each one of us shares in some way in the blessing and call of the apostles. We are all invited to love Jesus and become vessels of grace for God's honor. In Christ, with Christ, and through Christ, let us give glory to God and fulfill the call he has given to us.

Points for Meditation:

- Do you believe that, by virtue of your baptism, the Father and the Son live in you? If feelings of unworthiness cause you to doubt this truth, ask the Lord to show you how he has redeemed you through the cross. Pray that the Lord would manifest himself in you in a greater way.
- The *Catechism of the Catholic Church* teaches that the church "continues to be taught, sanctified, and guided by the apostles until Christ's return, through their successors"—the bishops, assisted by priests, in union with the successor of Peter, the pope (CCC, 857). Spend time interceding for the shepherds of the church. Ask that the

Lord fill them with wisdom and compassion in leading their flock to Christ.

When they discovered that they had been chosen, Simon and Jude must have felt not only honored, but also somewhat overwhelmed. Have you ever felt overwhelmed by a calling that God gave to you? What are some ways you can grow in confidence of God's calling for your life?

Prayer:

Lord Jesus, thank you for choosing men like Simon and Jude to build your church and for preserving their teachings for the past two thousand years. Thank you for the apostolate to which you have called us. Lord, come and make your home in us.

NOVEMBER 1

All Saints

Solemnity

Revelation 7:2-4,9-14
Psalm 24:1-6
1 John 3:1-3
Matthew 5:1-12

Who shall ascend the hill of the LORD? And who shall stand in his holy place? He who has clean hands and a pure heart.
(Psalm 24:3-4)

From the very beginning, the church has honored and revered its martyrs and heroes. What began on a popular and local level gradually became woven into the liturgy, beginning around the fourth century in the Eucharistic Prayer. In the fifth century, a feast honoring all the saints was declared in some Eastern churches, and from there the celebration was taken up in Rome. In 835, Pope Gregory

IV declared All Saints Day a feast for the entire church.

A day commemorating the saints is actually a day of rejoicing in the greatness of the Lord and hoping in his love. The victory that we see in the saints testifies to the Lord himself. It was not just their own efforts that produced such holiness, but the work of the Lord, who wants to pour the fullness of the life of Jesus into our hearts. This has been the hope and joy of all holy men and women always and everywhere, and it is our hope and joy as well.

The Book of Revelation contains a vision of the redeemed of the Lord, gathered around the throne of God: "They have washed their robes and made them white in the blood of the Lamb" (Revelation 7:14). The victory of the redeemed came through the blood of Jesus, which washed them, purified them, and sealed them with the promise of eternal life.

The power of this precious blood of Christ is available to us every day by faith. We can turn to Jesus at any moment and ask for his blood to cover our sins and cleanse us. We can call on Jesus at any moment for him to pour out the power of this death and resurrection to strengthen us and enable us to live as God's children. "What love the Father has given us, that we should be called children of God" (1 John 3:1). We are his children; he has adopted us as his very own! Every day, our Father's hand is extended to us and we have the great privilege to take hold of him.

Let us fix our eyes on the Lamb at the center of the throne who has promised to be our Shepherd and to lead us to "springs of living water" (Revelation 7:17). The Lord, who has worked in the lives of the saints, is ready to work in us if we will turn to him. Our God, who has chosen us to be his very own, is faithful!

Points for Meditation:

- Think of the saints whom you most admire. Then list the qualities they possessed that attract you. How did God use these character traits to make these men and women holy? How can he use your natural gifts and talents to help you grow in holiness?
- Spend some time meditating on the beatitudes (Matthew 5:1-12). Focus on the promises that Jesus makes to those who follow him. How are these promises—the kingdom of heaven, the vision of God, participation in the divine nature,

eternal life, and rest in God—a part of your every day decision-making? To what extent do they influence the goals you have for your life? On this day of grace and celebration, ask the Lord to give you a deeper desire to see his promises fulfilled in your life.

- Many saints led challenging and often painful lives, but still managed to retain their joy and love of the Lord because of their intimacy with Jesus. What are some concrete ways in which you can deepen your intimacy with the Lord?

Prayer:

Lord Jesus, the saints in heaven behold your glory and know the rewards of your life. Fill me with hope in your promise of eternal life. May we all share the joy of your saints in heaven.

NOVEMBER 2

Commemoration of All the Faithful Departed (All Souls)

Daniel 12:1-3
Psalm 103:8,10,13-18
Romans 6:3-9
John 6:37-40
(Many options available.)

For this is the will of my Father, that every one who sees the Son and believes in him should have eternal life; and I will raise him up at the last day. (John 6:40)

What tremendous love God has for us! What an amazing promise he has made: "As Christ was raised from the dead by the glory of the Father, we too might walk in newness of life" (Romans 6:4). When we were baptized, our old nature—marred through disobedience and defiled by sin—was joined to Jesus on the cross and died. Through baptism, St. Paul explains, we are buried with Jesus in his grave. Now, we can share in his victory over death. No longer enslaved to sin, we are transformed by the power of the Holy Spirit.

In our daily lives, however, we often fall short of the life we received in baptism. While tasting the new life of Christ, we act out of our old nature and give in to temptation and sin. This is why All Souls Day is so important. It reminds us that God, knowing the weakness and frailty of our human nature, has made a way for us to enter his holy presence perfectly cleansed and acceptable to him. As the church teaches, "All who die in God's grace and friendship, but still imperfectly purified, are indeed assured of their eternal salvation; but after death they undergo purification, so as to achieve the holiness necessary to enter the joy of heaven" (*Catechism of the Catholic Church*, 1030).

St. Catherine of Genoa once wrote: "Apart from the happiness of the saints in heaven, I think there is no joy comparable to that of the souls in purgatory" (*On Purgation and Purgatory*). Purgatory is not an antechamber of hell, one step short of damnation. Rather, it's the "waiting room" for heaven where we undergo a final cleaning up in order to appear before the all-holy God.

Can you imagine what it will be like when you're purified of all imperfections? When all love of self is transformed into love for God? Let's rejoice today in the power of the cross. By it, we and all those who have died in faith and baptism have been transformed. Together with all the saints, may we rejoice in the blessings of the life to come!

Points for Meditation:

- The tradition of the church is to pray for those who have passed on from this world. This kind of intercession is possible because of the union of all those who belong to Christ, a union that is not broken even by death. Spend some time today praying for family members and friends who have died. Pray that they may be purified and made ready to meet the Bridegroom face to face.
- Every Christian shares in Jesus' victory over death (Romans 6:9). As you think about the promise of eternal life and Jesus' commitment to bring about your total purification, ask the Spirit to fill you with an unshakable confidence in Christ.

Purification of our imperfections begins in this life as we respond to God's grace. Tell the Holy Spirit that you welcome his work of convicting you of sin and purifying you of all that cannot stand in the light of God's holiness. Thank him for his gifts of repentance and forgiveness.

Prayer:

Lord Jesus, by your cross and resurrection you overcame death and freed us from the power of sin. You have raised us up to new life. We rejoice today in the sure inheritance you have won for us!

NOVEMBER 9

Dedication of the St. John Lateran Basilica in Rome

Feast

Ezekiel 47:1-2,8-9,12
Psalm 84:3-6,8,11
1 Corinthians 3:9-11,16-17
John 2:13:22
(Many options available.)

Everything will live where the river goes. (Ezekiel 47:9)

Today we celebrate the Dedication of the Basilica of St. John Lateran. This building is the oldest and ranks the first among the four great basilicas in Rome (along with St. Peter's, St. Paul's, and St. Mary Major). It was donated to the church by the Emperor Constantine in 311, and since then it has been revered as the mother church of cathedrals everywhere. Over the centuries, the Basilica of St. John Lateran has suffered earthquake, fire, and invasion, and each time it was rebuilt, restored, and improved upon. Among the relics it houses is the wooden altar believed to be the original altar on which St. Peter celebrated Mass.

Why celebrate the dedication of a church building? We know that the church is more than a building, however ancient or venerable. Still, this man-made, stone basilica stands as a symbol of the church, the people of God. It is a reminder to us that the church is a temple, a place where God dwells and is worshipped by his people. This church can never be destroyed by natural disasters or vandalism. As Paul asked the early Christians in Corinth: "Do you not know that you are God's temple and that God's Spirit dwells in you?" (1 Corinthians 3:16).

On the cross, Jesus established his church as blood and water flowed from the temple of his body (John 19:34). In this healing flow, Ezekiel's vision of the new Jerusalem is fulfilled. Now, through the Holy Spirit, a great river flows from the church—the people of God—and brings life everywhere it goes. We are that temple, and from us can flow the healing and transforming power of the Spirit.

Today's anniversary reminds us of the power and wisdom of God which flows through Christ's church into the world. Let us pray for the whole church, that each of us would be sensitive to the Spirit of God and would cooperate with his desire to touch every person on earth.

Points for Meditation:

- As a cathedral, the Basilica of St. John Lateran symbolizes the unity of the local church—as all cathedrals do—and also the unity of the entire church. Ask the Lord to protect and strengthen the unity of the church so that it can continue to be a light to the world.
- Any place where the Lord's name is held sacred, and where his people live in obedience and love, carries a special blessing. This is true of every "domestic church"—every family that is set apart for the Lord. If you don't do so already, suggest to your family that you come together each day or week to pray. Include in your petitions the needs of families everywhere.
- Is there something you or your family can do to build up your own parish? Pray about whether God may be calling you to contribute your time or talent to your church. How may he want to use you to bring more of his life into your parish family?

Prayer:

Jesus, bring the river of living water to each of us in your church. Through us, bring healing to all the nations.

Christ the King

Solemnity

(Last Sunday in Ordinary Time)

Cycle A: Ezekiel 34:11-12,15-17
Psalm 23:1-3,5-6
1 Corinthians 15:20-25,28
Matthew 25:31-46

Cycle B: Daniel 7:13-14
Psalm 93:1-2,5
Revelation 1:5-8
John 18:33-37

Cycle C: 2 Samuel 5:1-3
Psalm 122:1-5
Colossians 1:12-20
Luke 23:35-43

When the Son of man comes in his glory, and all the angels with him, then he will sit on his glorious throne. (Matthew 25:31)

Scripture is rich in the imagery it uses to unveil Jesus: He is Lord, Servant, Master, Friend, Teacher, Prophet, Healer, and more. There is a wonderful depth to the person and mission of Christ which the Spirit longs to reveal to those who seek it. It is like the delight of an experienced jeweler who finds a prize diamond; like the joy of a new bride who cherishes every moment spent with her beloved. Today the church invites us to reflect on yet another aspect of Jesus' nature as we celebrate the feast of Christ the King.

Though Jesus is portrayed as king, he is neither haughty nor pompous. His kingship is tied intrinsically to the humble image of the good Shepherd. Throughout salvation history, Yahweh revealed himself as the faithful shepherd of his people (Genesis 49:24; Psalm 23:1; Isaiah 40:11). He promised to find his lost sheep and heal them, to feed them with justice (Ezekiel 34:11-16). Yahweh, the Father of Israel, fulfilled his promise by sending Jesus, who conquered our hearts through love, not power. Even so, the humble Christ is rightfully called king; he defeated death, and all creation is subject to him (1 Corinthians 15:26-28). As our king, he calls us to obey his law—the law of love.

Based on this law, he will require an accounting from us at the end of time: "Truly, I say to you, as you did it to one of the least of these my brethren, you did it to me" (Matthew 25:40).

How do we fulfill this law of love? Our own standards might leave us as bewildered as the goats in the parable. We must begin by humbly asking the King to reign in our hearts. For this reason, we come to the table of the Lord confessing: "Lord I am not worthy. . . . Only say the word and I shall be healed." As we receive Jesus' love for us into our hearts, we are empowered to serve others. If we receive openly, we can give generously.

Let us seek the green pastures of the Shepherd and allow him to fill our cup to overflowing. Then, at our journey's end, when Christ reigns over all creation, he will deliver us to the Father through the Spirit. He will commend us at last into the unity of the Trinity, saying: "Come, O blessed of my Father, inherit the kingdom prepared for you from the foundation of the world" (Matthew 25:34).

Points for Meditation:

- In Matthew 25, Jesus is described as coming in his glory and sitting on his royal throne. In separating the "sheep" from the "goats," what is this King most concerned about? How often do you recognize the King of glory disguised in the hungry, the homeless, the sick, or the imprisoned?

- Jesus is our King, but he never commands our allegiance. Instead, he waits for us to invite him to reign in our hearts. How is Jesus' kingship manifested in your life? Extend a fresh invitation to Jesus to reign more fully in your heart.
- If we are in the service of Christ the King, then we must be ready to advance his kingdom. Do you feel compelled to share the good news of Christ with others? Ask the Lord to give you a sense of urgency about evangelizing those who don't know him.

Prayer:

Jesus, I pray that when you return, you will find faith among all people. May your return find me feeding the hungry, welcoming strangers, and preaching your good news to all.

NOVEMBER 30

St. Andrew, apostle

Feast

Romans 10:9-18
Psalm 19:2-5
Matthew 4:18-22

How beautiful are the feet of those who preach good news! (Romans 10:15)

According to tradition, as he approached the instrument of his martyrdom, St. Andrew was heard to say, "O dearest cross honored as you have been by the body of my Master, long desired by me, my most cherished friend whom I sought constantly, . . . take me from men and give me to my Lord." Andrew's faith remained alive and strong as he faced his death.

Andrew had been a fisherman and disciple of John the Baptist before he began to follow Jesus. It is thought that Andrew was the first disciple to know

Jesus as the Messiah, the first to bring another to Jesus, and later, the first missionary. After being with Jesus for only a short time, Andrew was able to say with great confidence, "We have found the Messiah!" (John 1:41). This statement would not only bring his brother Simon Peter to Jesus, but many others as well.

Andrew saw Jesus heal the sick, overpower demons with a word, and forgive people's sins. He saw Jesus multiply the loaves and fishes and raise Lazarus from the dead. Finally, he saw Jesus, once crucified, standing before him alive by the power of the Spirit. It was this very Spirit who, after Pentecost, burned so brightly in Andrew's heart that it could not be contained. Compelled by the Spirit, Andrew traveled far and wide proclaiming, "Jesus is Lord." He preached in Southern Russia and along the shores of the Black Sea and in Byzantium (modern-day Istanbul). Andrew was convinced that the same things that Jesus had done in Galilee and Jerusalem, he was charged to do all over the world by the power of the Holy Spirit.

Andrew knew that evangelization is not just a matter of convincing people of the rightness of theological propositions. It's also a matter of revealing the glory of Christ by healing the sick, forgiving our enemies, and loving everyone with the love of Christ. Let us take up our calling as Andrew did and bring the word of God to everyone we know.

Points for Meditation:

- Andrew was a disciple of John the Baptist before he joined Jesus. In following first John and then Jesus, what do you think he was looking for? Imagine yourself for a moment in the shoes of the fisherman Andrew. What is it about Jesus that makes you so sure that he truly is the Messiah?
- When Jesus called, Andrew responded immediately, leaving everything else behind. What are some practical and immediate ways that you can respond to Jesus' call in your life? Is there a broken relationship you can mend? Is there someone you can serve who is in need? Is there someone with whom you should share the gospel? Are you called to love a family member in a more sacrificial way?
- Andrew's heart burned with love for Jesus, to the point that he was honored to share in the same death on the cross. Do you desire to

love Jesus more intensely? Ask the Lord to fill your heart with love for your Savior.

Prayer:

Lord Jesus, manifest your glory in my life. I believe that the resurrection is real and that you have commissioned me to be a messenger of your gospel. By your Spirit empower me, as you did Andrew, to tell the world about the freedom it so desperately needs.

DECEMBER 8

Immaculate Conception

Solemnity

Genesis 3:9-15,20
Psalm 98:1-4
Ephesians 1:3-6,11-12
Luke 1:26-38

The man called his wife's name Eve, because she was the mother of all living. (Genesis 3:20)

On this feast of the Immaculate Conception, we read the story of our first parents' fall and God's promise of salvation through an offspring of Eve. As he read this passage, St. Jerome (342-420) understood that a new Eve would be the one to crush the head of the serpent. Like the first Eve, she too would be called the "mother of all the living," because she would give birth to the Living One who would deliver us from death and create anew all who believed in him.

Mary's immaculate conception marked the beginning of this new creation in Christ. Just as God created everything at the beginning, so now with Mary he began his wondrous act of re-creating everything, renewing the entire heaven and earth through the redemption that her son would accomplish. Throughout the ages, Mary has been recognized as the new Eve whose "yes" undid the "no" of the first Eve, just as Jesus is the new Adam who ushered in a new life for God's people. In her humility and faithfulness, Mary stands as a sign of this new creation.

On this feast, we look particularly at the holiness of Mary who, in a unique way, was "chosen before the foundation of the world to be holy and blameless" before God (Ephesians 1:4). Mary was particularly open to the Holy Spirit. Her words, "Let it be to me according to your word" (Luke 1:38), represent a profound consecration that was never taken back, but only deepened throughout her life.

May each of us allow God's Spirit to remove any obstacles that would hinder his action in our lives. May we all respond to him with a perfect "yes," as Mary did, and so know God's blessing and favor. Just as God is renewing the whole of creation, he wants to renew each of us.

Points for Meditation:

- Mary's immaculate conception was carefully planned by the Father so that she could become a perfect vessel for his Son. As with Mary, God has planned every detail of your life. Look back on a particularly difficult time and ask the Spirit to help you see how this trial fit into God's plan for your growth in Christ. Let this reflection give you a greater trust for the future that "in everything God works for good with those who love him, who are called according to his purpose" (Romans 8:28).
- When Mary questioned how she, a virgin, would become pregnant, the angel Gabriel answered, "With God nothing will be impossible" (Luke 1:37). Are you facing a problem that seems impossible to resolve? Ask the Lord to fill you with hope that with him, nothing is impossible.
- In his Letter to the Ephesians, St. Paul said that we who hope in Christ "have been destined and appointed to live for the praise of his glory" (1:12). Mary lived for the praise of God's glory. How does your life reflect the glory of God? How can you better live for the "praise of God's glory"?

Prayer:

Father, we ask that you continue to re-create us in your image and likeness. Help us to be like Mary, who humbly embraced your will and rejoiced in your love. Fill us with your presence, as we look forward to the day when we will see you face to face.

DECEMBER 12

Our Lady of Guadalupe

Memorial

Zechariah 2:14-17 (2:10-13, RSV)
Psalm 45:11-12,14-17
Luke 1:39-47
(Many options available.)

Sing and rejoice, O daughter of Zion; for lo, I come and I will dwell in the midst of you, says the LORD. *(Zechariah 2:10, RSV)*

The feast of Our Lady of Guadalupe reminds us that God is Lord of history, for Mary's appearance at Guadalupe lifted the church over a seemingly insurmountable obstacle and radically changed the course of history in the Americas.

By the 1400s, God had enabled Christian Europe to advance in science and technology to the point where Europeans became the first people to travel around the world. God's chief concern undoubtedly was that they would spread the gospel in humility and love. Many missionaries who followed the explorers did just that. However, many of the European traders, military men, and adventurers were much more interested in carving out colonial empires and gaining glory and gold than in serving God. Their scandalous violation of the gospel became an enormous barrier to evangelism.

This was especially true in Mexico where, after Spain conquered the Aztecs around 1520, missionaries were able to make very little headway. In 1531, however, a devout peasant named Juan Diego had a vision of the Virgin Mary. To convince the bishop that the vision was real, Mary supplied Juan Diego with a bouquet of out-of-season roses. Even more astonishing, a miraculous image of herself appeared on the inside of Juan Diego's tilma or cloak. Portraying Mary as a saintly girl crushing a serpent, the image was filled with symbolism that spoke powerfully to the Aztecs of God's mercy. Before long, thousands of Aztecs turned to Christ.

Jesus is still capable of revealing himself in power. Through Mary's appearance, God made himself known to a pagan people and touched off a great revival in a nation in darkness and idolatry. What is your vision of God? Is he big enough to bring millions to Jesus in a short time? Don't limit him by unbelief. Pray, intercede, and expect miracles. His desire—and his power—to bring all his children back to him is as strong today as it was in 1531.

Points for Meditation:

- The coloring and technique of the portrait of Mary on Juan Diego's tilma remain mysteries. The colors have never faded, nor has the coarse fabric woven from cactus fiber ever deteriorated. If you can, obtain a copy of this image. Note the details, including the fact that Mary is depicted as an Indian girl. Think of how dearly our Father in heaven loves his creation, that he would show his glory in such a concrete way in order to bring a people to himself.
- Over the centuries, Mary's powerful intercession and her appearances in the world have led to countless conversions. As mother of the church, ask her to intercede for the success and power of evangelization efforts all over the world, both in those places where Christ is unknown and in those where the faith needs to be renewed and revived.

Our Lady of Guadalupe is the patroness of the Catholic pro-life movement. Intercede for the protection of all unborn babies. Ask the Lord to change the hearts of men and women everywhere so that they would see the wonders of his creation and value every human being who is made in his image and likeness.

Prayer:

Sovereign Lord, you once sent Mary to open the way for the gospel in Mexico. Open the way for the gospel in our day. By your Spirit, strike down the evils of our time and usher in a mighty wave of revival in our nation and to all the ends of the earth.

DECEMBER 25

Nativity of the Lord (Christmas)

Solemnity

Vigil:
Isaiah 62:1-5
Psalm 89:4-5,16-17,27,29
Acts 13:16-17,22-25
Matthew 1:1-25

Mass at Midnight:
Isaiah 9:1-6
Psalm 96:1-3,11-13
Titus 2:11-14
Luke 2:1-14

Mass during the Day:
Isaiah 52:7-10
Psalm 98:1-6
Hebrews 1:1-6
John 1:1-18

And the Word became flesh,
and dwelt among us. (John 1:14)

The greatest gift you have is your life. But this gift is also a mystery, something that we can't completely figure out on our own. How do you unwrap a mystery? The answer is found wrapped in a manger, in the mystery of the one who is fully God and fully man. As we unwrap the mystery of Jesus' life, the mystery of our own lives will make more and more sense.

Scripture tells us that from all eternity, Jesus, the Word, was with God and that he was God (John 1:1). This Word became flesh and lived among us. But why did he choose to come among us? A clue is found in his name, Yeshua, which means "God saves." In Jesus, God has come among us to save us, to rescue us.

From what did Jesus come to save us? He saved us from the death that entered the world when our first parents embraced the lies and envy of the devil (Wisdom 2:23-24). We were created to become like Jesus in all his purity and holiness, but because of sin, our vision became clouded. Restlessly, we search for what might increase our happiness and satisfy the desires of our hearts. But we pursue narrow goals. We strive to fill our lives with meaning and still do not feel complete. There, resting in the manger, is the "Bread of Life," the only one who can satisfy our hunger.

Take a moment to think of all that this infant child of Bethlehem means. His coming among us as man is the fulcrum of all God's action, the center from which all his blessings flow out to us.

Imagine: If God had only created us in his image, that would have been enough. If he had only sent us his word through the prophets, that would have been enough. If he had only come among us to comfort us and teach us a new way to live, that would have been enough. If he had only forgiven our sins, that would have been enough. If he had only sent his Spirit to guide the church, that would have been enough. But God has done all these things and more. He has given us Christ himself to live in our hearts. He has promised us that Jesus will return to take us into his glory.

In the incarnation of his Son, God restored every blessing we forfeited when we fell into sin. From the very beginning, the Son of God was destined to be the source and goal of our lives. In love, God made us like himself, with the powers of intellect, emotion, and will. In love, he placed within us a hunger for himself. How could he help but do everything in his power to satisfy that hunger—even to the point of sacrificing his only Son for our sake?

This is a day of great rejoicing, for our destiny has been restored! As we look into the manger, we see innocence, purity, and divine life. This seemingly vulnerable child is the way of our salvation. He died for our sins, was raised for our justification, and will come again to judge the living and the dead. In a sense, the manger is a mirror of our lives, for there we see the glorious power of the indestructible life that God has intended for all of us.

Points for Meditation:

- What you do see when you look into the manger? Let your heart rejoice over the good news that this child has restored you to God. Ask the Spirit to show you the depths of the riches of Christ, your greatest Christmas gift.
- Jesus was born impoverished, placed in an animal's stall, and wrapped in swaddling clothes. Why do you think the Father would plan such a lowly appearance for the Word, who had been with him from all time? Reflect on the extent to which Jesus would go to save humanity.
- The church speaks of the "marvelous exchange" —man's Creator has become man, and we have become sharers in the divinity of Christ who humbled himself to share our humanity (*Catechism of the Catholic Church*, 526). As you meditate on the reality of this "marvelous

exchange," imagine the baby Jesus offering you his gift of divine life.

Prayer:

Heavenly Father, thank you for the gift of life, and for the gift of your Son in whom we have eternal life. By your Spirit, reveal to me the treasures held in the incarnation. Move me to love today, even if I do not feel like loving. Teach me to live like this child, who teaches us that to give is to receive.

DECEMBER 26

St. Stephen, first martyr

Feast

Acts 6:8-10; 7:54-59
Psalm 31:3-4,6-8,17,21
Matthew 10:17-22

When they deliver you up, do not be anxious how you are to speak or what you are to say; for what you are to say will be given to you in that hour; for it is not you who speak, but the Spirit of your Father speaking through you. (Matthew 10:19-20)

After all the celebrations of the Prince of Peace, we are faced with the tale of the first Christian martyr. How sobering a shift! We are called to acknowledge that the peace Jesus came to give us was won at a very dear price: his blood, and the blood of all the martyrs down through the ages.

From the very beginning, we learn that true peace can only come as we embrace the one who died in our place and allow his cross to penetrate our lives.

How wonderfully did Stephen reflect these truths! As he told Stephen's story, Luke placed special emphasis on Stephen's resemblance to Jesus. He was full of grace and power; he performed great signs and wonders; he spoke with the wisdom of the Spirit (Acts 6:8,10). As he was being executed, he prayed: "Receive my spirit" (7:59); and he forgave: "Lord, do not hold this sin against them" (7:60).

This is why Jesus came: to make us into children of God filled with the power of the Holy Spirit. When we repent and are baptized, we too receive the Spirit. As we go about our daily lives, however, it's not uncommon for distractions and worldly concerns to consume us. Sin, the influences of Satan, and desires for the things of the world can occupy our hearts so quickly. This is why we need to pray daily: "Come, Holy Spirit. Fill us, transform us, make us more like Jesus."

Everything that Stephen and all the early disciples experienced is available to us today. Let us invite the Lord to work more deeply in our lives. Let him free you from sin; give him more room in your heart; spend a little more time pondering his word; open your heart a little more when you receive him in the Eucharist. These are all ways we can place ourselves at the Spirit's disposal and be filled to overflowing with the life and love of God. Filled with the Spirit as Stephen was, we too will reflect the glory of God and become bold proclaimers of the gospel.

Points for Meditation:

- Stephen was chosen, with six other men, to wait on tables (Acts 6:2-5) to ensure that all Christians in need were fed. We don't know anything more about this early Christian except that he was "full of faith and of the Holy Spirit" (6:5). Do you believe that God wants to make you, like Stephen, "full of faith and of the Holy Spirit"? Right now, ask God to give you more of his Holy Spirit. Pray with all your heart for the Lord to fill you with even greater faith.
- Martyrs are able to trust God in the face of death because they have experienced God's faithfulness and power throughout their lives. Recall times in your life when you have seen God's faithfulness and power manifested. Even if you never face physical martyrdom, how will these expe-

riences help you as you face the prospect of passing from this life to the next?

- Stephen "did great wonders and signs among the people" (Acts 6:8). Do you expect to see miracles happen even today? Build up your faith by reading about some modern-day "signs and wonders." Come to expect them as part of your life in Christ.

Prayer:

Holy Spirit, fill us as you filled your first followers. Make us more like Jesus. Empower us to do the good works that you have intended for us to do.

DECEMBER 27

St. John, apostle and evangelist

Feast

1 John 1:1-4
Psalm 97:1-2,5-6,11-12
John 20:2-8

Then the other disciple, who reached the tomb first, also went in, and he saw and believed. (John 20:8)

What an immense privilege to be at Jesus' tomb on the day he rose from the dead! Yet John believed even before he saw the risen Christ. He only saw the burial cloths and the empty tomb—and he believed. From the evidence before him, he accepted the gift of faith that God offered him at that moment (John 20:4-8). In this way, John is an example for us, for the gift of faith that he was given is available to all.

Certainly John lived an extraordinarily graced life. He saw, touched, and heard Jesus, the "word of life" (1 John 1:1). Yet John had to exercise faith that Jesus was the Messiah and Son of God. He also had to learn the humility and obedience that are a necessary part of the Christian life. The good news is that the same Spirit that enabled John to believe in Jesus has been given to us as well.

Actually, we have more evidence of Jesus' lordship and resurrection than John had in his time. We have two thousand years of Christian history testifying to the power of the risen Christ in transformed lives. When we consider the testimony of faith over the centuries and the evidence of Christian faith among the millions of people today who count themselves as Christians, we can be strengthened in our own faith in ways unavailable to John in his day. Even when the church has been beset by the weakness and sins of its members, the light of holiness has endured, bearing witness to the risen Christ even in the darkest of moments.

It is right, then, for our belief in Jesus' resurrection to be more than intellectual. With so much evidence of his resurrection, we can place our whole hearts and lives in the hands of the risen Savior. He loves us immensely. He has called us to be his beloved disciples, just as certainly as he called John. He wants to shower us with his grace in ways that will bring us as much wonder and joy as John experienced as he peered into the empty tomb.

Points for Meditation:

- None of the disciples seemed prepared for Jesus' resurrection, even though Jesus himself had, on several occasions, spoken of it (Matthew 17:23; Luke 9:22). Yet when John saw the empty tomb, everything suddenly made sense to him. How have you experienced the risen Christ? Try to find some specific ways, such as prayer, Scripture, and the sacraments, to prepare your heart each day for the risen Christ to manifest himself through you.
- John knew Jesus as he came in the flesh and walked among the people of his time, but more importantly, he knew the Lord Jesus after his resurrection. Read through the first Letter of John. Take note of how often his preaching alludes to the reality of the risen Christ.
- John says that a test of whether we love God is whether we love our brothers and sisters (1 John

4:20-21). Is there someone in your life with whom you are struggling to love? Forgive that person from the bottom of your heart. Ask God to replace your anger and hurt with his love.

Prayer:

Jesus, Redeemer of the world, I love you and praise you. Thank you for coming to give me life. Thank you for the precious gift of faith in you.

DECEMBER 28

Holy Innocents, martyrs

Feast

1 John 1:5–2:2
Psalm 124:2-5,7-8
Matthew 2:13-18

An angel of the Lord appeared to Joseph in a dream and said, "Rise, take the child and his mother, and flee to Egypt, and remain there till I tell you; for Herod is about to search for the child, to destroy him."
(Matthew 2:13)

Worldly powers did not take long to oppose Jesus! Mary and Joseph were rejoicing over their newborn son when suddenly, they were forced to flee during the night to a foreign land to protect the child who would save the world.

Scholars believe that about twenty male babies were slaughtered by King Herod's forces. These children were among the first to gain entrance into paradise. As the opening prayer for this feast says to God our Father: "The Holy Innocents offered you praise by the death they suffered for Christ."

This feast reminds us that although the powers of darkness rage against the light of Christ, Jesus is always the victor. Through the dream given to Joseph, the Holy Family was able to keep Jesus safe. The babies that died are honored as martyrs by the church, and today they sing in heaven the praises of their rightful King. "The light shines in the darkness, and the darkness has not overcome it" (John 1:5).

For centuries, saints and scholars have compared Herod's rage against the children of Bethlehem to the devil's rage against the children of God. Just as Herod perceived Jesus as a rival to his kingship, so Satan sees us as a threat to his influence in the world. What could be more frightening to Satan than the thought of men and women in every nation filled with the grace and power of the Holy Spirit? No wonder he seeks to destroy our faith and trust in Jesus!

Scripture calls us to take up the weapons of God and engage in the spiritual battle every day (Ephesians 6:10-17). We have the word of God as a sword capable of cutting through the lies of the devil, and faith in Jesus as a shield against the devil's flaming darts. By protecting our minds with the truth of our salvation in Christ, we can bring our thoughts and actions into obedience with Jesus. We need never fear the devil. No matter how insidious he is, Jesus is infinitely more powerful. Let us rest in Christ and allow him to abide in our hearts.

Points for Meditation:

- Satan often works by sowing doubt in our minds about God's word, hoping that we will water down the gospel. Have you entertained thoughts that your sins really aren't all that bad, or that it's okay to give in to a little temptation? If you are harboring such thoughts now, see them as tricks of the devil. Resist any temptations to set lower standards for yourself.
- King Herod felt threatened by the birth of one rumored to be the new king of the Jews because he was afraid of losing his kingdom. Thus, he could not receive what God wanted to give him

because he couldn't bear the thought of losing what he had. To receive the kingdom, we must relinquish anything that keeps us from Jesus, our true King. Ask the Lord to show you any lesser loves you have that might be interfering with surrendering your life freely to him.

- The feast of the Holy Innocents points to the truth that Christians will suffer in this life just as Jesus did. If you are undergoing suffering right now, ask God to help you see the fruit your suffering will bear, for yourself and for others. Ask God to help you persevere with joy, knowing that he will never abandon you.

Prayer:

Father, thank you for the gift of salvation. Help me to stay close to you and obey you. Let me hear your Holy Spirit speaking to me and directing my paths, so that I may always walk in your light. Thank you for your love and protection.

Holy Family

Feast

(Sunday in the Octave of Christmas)

Sirach 3:2-6,12-14
Psalm 128:1-5
Colossians 3:12-21
Cycle A: Matthew 2:13-15,19-23
Cycle B: Luke 2:22-40
Cycle C: Luke 2:41-52

Put on love, which binds everything together in perfect harmony. (Colossians 3:14)

St. Paul's words on the Christ-like way we are to treat one another are often read at wedding liturgies because they offer sound advice for couples embarking on a lifetime commitment. Compassion, kindness, meekness, forbearance, forgiveness—all bound by love—reflect the "putting on" of Christ that is every family's calling (Colossians 3:12).

Born "on the road" and raised in a humble home in Nazareth, Jesus is intimately connected to family life. Through the power of the Holy Spirit, he wants to live in our families, giving us the grace we need to reflect his love to each other. The more we invite Christ into our homes through family prayer and Scripture reading, times of recreation together, and an atmosphere of love and acceptance, the more we will be able live out these inspired words.

In his *Letter to Families* (February 2, 1994), Pope John Paul II commented on the role of simple family life in God's plan of salvation:

> The family has its origins in that same love with which the Creator embraces the created world. . . . We know that the Redeemer spent most of his life in the obscurity of Nazareth, "obedient" as the "Son of Man" to Mary his Mother, and to Joseph the carpenter. Is this filial "obedience" of Christ not already the first expression of that obedience to the Father "unto death" whereby he redeemed the world? (*Letter to Families*, 2)

Like all families, and more keenly than most, the Holy Family experienced trials and needed to rely continually on God's love and providence.

When Simeon prophesied that a sword would pierce her heart (Luke 2:29-35), Mary could only guess at the suffering her family would endure. Yet she and Joseph continued to be open to God's will for them, faithfully carrying out the duties entrusted to them.

These duties were most often the small, humble tasks required of any parent: comforting and caring for a child who had skinned his knee, cooking and cleaning, teaching him to pray. Simple acts though they were, they were all done for God's glory. In the same way, we can serve our families by immersing ourselves in Christ and seeking to love them as if we were loving him.

Points for Meditation:

- Think of the routine but necessary duties you perform for you family. How often do you consider these duties as acts of love? As you go about your chores over the next few days, think of how much you love the family members you are serving. Think of yourself as building God's kingdom and bringing him glory, even in the smallest and humblest of tasks.

- Read Colossians 3:12-21 as an examination of conscience. Ask the Holy Spirit to show you if there is any need for repentance in the way you serve your family. Ask God to help you reflect his love in every situation.
- Single parents have a huge burden in raising children on their own. If you know of any single-parent families, offer to help them. If you are a single parent, ask God to help you find good Christian friends willing to lend you a helping hand. Above all, pray for all single families, that Christ would make their burdens light.

Prayer:

Lord, help us to reflect your sacrificial love to our families. By your Spirit, transform our family into a reflection of your love.

Also from The Word Among Us Press:

The Wisdom Series:

Welcoming the New Millennium: Wisdom from Pope John Paul II
My Heart Speaks: Wisdom from Pope John XXIII
Live Jesus! Wisdom from Saints Francis de Sales and Jane de Chantal
A Radical Love: Wisdom from Dorothy Day
Walking with the Father: Wisdom from Brother Lawrence
Touching the Risen Christ: Wisdom from The Fathers
Love Songs: Wisdom from Saint Bernard of Clairvaux

These popular books include short biographies of the authors and selections from their writings grouped around themes such as prayer, forgiveness, and mercy.

The New Testament Devotional Commentary Series:

Matthew: A Devotional Commentary
Mark: A Devotional Commentary
Luke: A Devotional Commentary
John: A Devotional Commentary
Acts of the Apostles: A Devotional Commentary
Leo Zanchettin, General Editor

Enjoy praying through the New Testament with commentaries that include each passage of scripture with a faith-filled meditation.

Books on Saints:

A Great Cloud of Witnesses: The Stories of 16 Saints and Christian Heroes by Leo Zanchettin and Patricia Mitchell

I Have Called You by Name: The Stories of 16 Saints and Christian Heroes by Patricia Mitchell

Each book contains inspiring biographies, along with selections of the saints' own writings.